Confronting Poverty in Iraq

Confronting Poverty in Iraq

Main Findings

THE WORLD BANK
WASHINGTON, D.C.

PERMANENT TECHNICAL COMMITTEE
FOR POVERTY REDUCTION POLICIES,
THE REPUBLIC OF IRAQ

© **2011** The International Bank for Reconstruction and Development / The World Bank
1818 H Street, NW
Washington, DC 20433
Telephone: 202-473-1000
Internet: www.worldbank.org

This volume is a product of the staff of the International Bank for Reconstruction and Development / The World Bank. The findings, interpretations, and conclusions expressed in this volume do not necessarily reflect the views of the Executive Directors of The World Bank or the governments they represent.

The World Bank does not guarantee the accuracy of the data included in this work. The boundaries, colors, denominations, and other information shown on any map in this work do not imply any judgement on the part of The World Bank concerning the legal status of any territory or the endorsement or acceptance of such boundaries.

ISBN: 978-0-8213-8562-3
eISBN: 978-0-8213-8563-0
DOI: 10.1596/978-0-8213-8562-3

Cover images: COSIT, Iraq

Library of Congress Cataloging-in-Publication Data

Confronting poverty in Iraq : main findings.
    p. cm.
 "Poverty Reduction Strategy High Committee Government of Iraq."
 Includes bibliographical references.
 ISBN 978-0-8213-8562-3 -- ISBN 978-0-8213-8563-0 (electronic)
 1. Poverty--Iraq. 2. Poor--Iraq. 3. Cost and standard of living--Iraq. 4. Iraq--Economic conditions.
I. World Bank. II. Iraq. Poverty Reduction Strategy High Committee.
 HC415.4.Z9P637 2010
 339.4'609567--dc22

                                               2010032695

Contents

List of Tables

List of Figures

List of Boxes

Foreword

Iraq began its reconstruction journey in 2003 with a destination but without a roadmap. The destination was a free society and an open, productive economy that would benefit all Iraqis. Yet not only was the map missing but also the key elements necessary to draw one—information, analysis, and a strategy on how to get there.

This book reports upon the analysis element of the multiyear process to create that missing map. This effort has been led since 2006 by the Poverty Reduction Strategy High Committee (PRSHC) of Iraq, a high-level technical working group whose distinguished members represent Iraq's parliament, its academic community, and virtually every government ministry involved in issues of social welfare. PRSHC has succeeded in a formidable three-fold challenge: to develop a foundation of reliable information that can be used to describe, understand, and assess the welfare of the entire population of Iraq; to analyze that information in a balanced, objective, and rigorous fashion; and to devise, based on that analysis, a thoughtful strategy for poverty reduction.

The roadmap has emerged through three phases of effort. First, a systematic yearlong field study was carried out to provide a foundation of basic data as a starting point. The Iraq Household Socio-Economic Survey (IHSES) in 2006-07 was the most comprehensive socioeconomic survey ever undertaken in Iraq. It generated high-quality data covering virtually every aspect of household income and expenditure. It surveyed more than18,000 households (about 127,000 individuals).

The richness of IHSES data goes well beyond demographic description and economic activity of the population. The data provide an up-to-date view at the national level of physical living conditions, food consumption, health, and education, as well as noneconomic activities of Iraq's population. The new information has and will prove useful beyond poverty analysis—for example, updating the outdated consumer price index (CPI). A statistical baseline has also been created against which future progress in poverty reduction can be monitored, evaluated, and further refined.

Second, in-depth analysis was carried out on the characteristics, causes, and consequences of poverty, an effort that was launched with six thematic papers in 2008. PRSHC addressed the complex issue of how poverty should be defined and measured; and a technical subcommittee was then assigned to establish an Iraq-specific poverty line. This initial conceptual work was crucial, because a precise definition of who is and is not poor served as the basis for all subsequent statistical work on productive activities, consumption, geographic distribution, education, health, and living conditions of the poor. The poverty line definition derived for the IHSES data was adopted by the Council of Ministers, thus creating a shared metric for future policymaking and program planning.

Third, in-depth analysis was followed by a process of deliberation and consultation with stakeholders about priority interventions for poverty reduction. Six key areas of action were identified; options debated; and concrete strategy proposals emerged—including, most importantly, short- and medium-term budget recommendations based on the selected priorities and realism in budgetary assessment. On November 24, 2009, the National Strategy for Poverty Reduction was adopted by the Council of Ministers; and on January 19, 2010, it was presented to the Council of Representatives.

The new national strategy is groundbreaking. It refocuses social welfare expenditure away from massive government subsidies for consumption, primarily through universal food rations, and redirects it in two directions—first, expanded investment in human productivity; and second, targeted (though significantly increased)transfers to the poor. The new strategy aims to increase the earnings capacity of the Iraqi population and to improve protection for those who are unable to earn enough through their labor. It focuses particular attention on productivity investments that will benefit the majority of the population who live close to the poverty line, as well as women—a group that is disproportionately outside the labor force. The groundbreaking poverty reduction strategy is anchored in parallel new thinking on a broader economic development strategy for Iraq—to replace the current overdependence on oil with a stable, diversified economy that generates well-paying jobs and entrepreneurial opportunities at every level of society.

Confronting Poverty in Iraq culminates the second step—that is, the analysis stage. The document is divided into two parts. The main findings summarize key conclusions and central messages without digression into the massive documentation and technical detail. Corresponding explanations of methodology and supplementary evidence are provided in the supplementary reference section, which is organized in parallel but only available online. Considerable comparative data are included throughout on how Iraq compares with neighboring countries in the Middle East and North Africa and other lower-middle-income countries.

The supplementary volume is broken down more finely—by Iraqi governorate, urban–rural location, poverty status, income level, expenditure level, gender, education, and so forth. The large quantity of detail is also intended to provide a reference function. Much new information has been produced through this research, including the national-level perspective that was heretofore unavailable. It is hoped that the abundance of new statistical materials will provide policymakers and researchers with fresh perspectives and many new entry points for extending and deepening the present analysis.

The richness of this document reflects the collegial and exceptionally productive working relationship between the Government of Iraq and the World Bank. Many more individuals and institutions must be thanked than can be named in this short foreword. However, on the government side, the lead role was played by the Central Organization for Statistics and Information Technology (COSIT) of Iraq with the Kurdistan Region Statistics Organization (KRSO) working as a strong operational partner to carry out this research. Their fruitful collaboration has produced the first unified statistical overview of all of Iraq's governorates and the entire national population.

The quality of IHSES data and the rigor of this analytical document strongly attest to institutional strengthening that has taken place in Iraq over the past few years. It should be noted that the Data Analysis Unit of COSIT, which assumed increasing responsibility for data management and the technical analysis, did not exist when this initiative was conceived in late 2003.

On the World Bank side, this effort has been managed by the Social and Economic Department of the Middle East and North Africa (MENA) region. The Bank team was led by Dr. Susan Razzaz, who served as an intellectual partner and was the key liaison to mobilize technical assistance and training.

Financial support was received through the generosity of donors to the Iraq Trust Fund (ITF) administered by the World Bank. The research described here was carried out under the Household Survey and Policies for Poverty Reduction (HSPPR) project. Financing included a US$5.5 million grant to the Ministry of Planning and Development Cooperation (MOPDC) as well as a US$3.6 million grant for the technical assistance executed by the Bank.

As in any undertaking of this magnitude, there are more contributors and intellectual authors than can be adequately recognized. However, one person, above all, must be singled out here. The director of the IHSES, Louay Haqqi Rashid, was assassinated in the course of his service to this project. This cruel and brutal act deprived Louay of the pleasure of seeing this latest fruit from his effort. Yet his sacrifice is well remembered by his many friends and colleagues—a symbol not just of his own commitment to a better future for Iraq, but to the countless individuals who have picked up the challenge and are carrying his work forward.

Dr. Mehdi M. Al-Alak, Chair
Poverty Reduction Strategy High
Committee; and
Director, Central Organization for
Statistics and Information Technology
(COSIT)

Hedi Larbi, Director
Middle East Department
The World Bank

Preface

This report is a joint undertaking of the Central Organization for Statistics and Information Technology (COSIT) of Iraq, the Kurdistan Region Statistics Organization (KRSO), and the International Bank for Reconstruction and Development/The World Bank. The findings, interpretations, and conclusions expressed in this work do not necessarily reflect the views of the Government of the Republic of Iraq, the Executive Directors of the World Bank, or the governments that the Executive Directors represent. The Bank, the Government of Iraq, and the governments represented do not guarantee the accuracy of the data included here. The boundaries, s, and denominations on maps do not imply judgments concerning the legal status of any territories shown.

Electronic copies of both volumes of this work—Main Findings and Reference Materials—can be downloaded at no charge in Arabic and in English from www.cosit.gov.iq and from www.worldbank.org/iq. Much of the analysis in this work is based on the Iraq Household Socio-Economic Survey (IHSES). An IHSES data CD can be obtained at no charge upon request from the Department of Public Relations and Dissemination, Central Organization for Statistics and Information Technology (COSIT), Elwiya (Elwiya Communications Office), Baghdad, Iraq; or http://go.worldbank.org/PW5WDSCHZO. The eBook version of the Main Findings can be found at http://go.worldbank.org/6M9ANGOF60.

Contributors and Acknowledgments

The Poverty Reduction Strategy High Committee (PRSHC) is the primary Iraqi entity responsible for the poverty analysis. PRSHC was convened by His Excellency Dr. Barham Salih, Minister of Planning and Development Cooperation (MOPDC) on September 16, 2006, and includes representatives nominated from a wide range of institutions by their respective heads. PRSHC prepared the National Poverty Reduction Strategy, which was officially adopted by the Council of Ministers of Iraq on November 24, 2009. The World Bank participated in this initiative as a provider of technical assistance and collaborator in the research. The present report represents a collaborative effort in every respect.

The Government of Iraq Team

The Poverty Reduction Strategy High Committee (PRSHC)
(as of December 2009)

Dr. Mehdi Muhsin Al Alak, Chairman, PRSHC; Undersecretary, MOPDC, Head, Central Organization for Statistics and Information Technology (COSIT)

Dr. Amira Mohammed Hussain, Member of Parliament

Dr. Abida Ahmed Dakhil, Member of Parliament

Ala'a Abdullah Al-Sa'doon, Member of Parliament

Hussain Mansour Al-Safi, Undersecretary, Ministry of Justice

Zeki Abdul Wahab Al-Jadir, Director of Project Implementation Team

Dr. Abdullah Al-Bandar, Adviser on the Advisory Commission, Office of the Prime Minister

Dr. Ali Al-Zubaidi, Director General, Ministry of Education

Dr. Ihasn Ja'afer Ahmed, Director General, Ministry of Health

Riadh Fakher Khalaf Al-Hashimi, Director General, Ministry of Trade

Layla Kadhim Aziz, Director General, Ministry of Labor and Social Affairs

Mahmood Othman Ma'aroof, Adviser, Ministry of Planning, Kurdistan Region

Dr. Jamal Rasool Mohammed Ameen, Adviser, Ministry of Planning, Kurdistan Region

Nidhal Abdul Karim Jawad, Representative of the Ministry of Finance

Najah Jalil Khalil, Assistant Director General, Ministry of Labor and Social Affairs, Kurdistan Region

Dr. Karim Mohammed Hamza, Academic Specialist, Baghdad University

Najla' Ali Murad, Director of the Living Conditions Statistics Department, COSIT

Abdullah Hasan Mathi, Deputy Project Director

PRSHC Advisory Team

Dr. Amal Shlash, Head of Advisory Team, Beit-al-Hikma

Dr. Karim Mohammed Hamza, Academic Specialist, Baghdad University

Dr. Hassan Latif Al-Zubaidi, Kufa University

Poverty Analysis Technical Committee

Uqood Hussein Salman Al Saad, Human Development Office, MOPDC

Nawal Abbas Mahdi, Human Development Office, MOPDC

Hassan Ahmmad K, Business Administration and Economics, Babil University

Nahidah Abdulkareem Abdul Hafedh, Department of Sociology, Baghdad University

Thanaa Abbas Salman Hilmi, Human Development Statistics, COSIT

Khawla Ali Mohammed, Human Development Office, MOPDC

Faris Al-Lami, College of Medicine, Baghdad University

Muna Attallah Ali, Primary Health Department, Public Health Office, Ministry of Health

Wafaa Jafar Al Mahdawi, College of Administration and Economics, Al-Mustansiriyah University

Abdulwahid Mishaal Abed, Sociology Department, Baghdad University

Poverty Line Committee

Raghdaa Dheyaa Sadeq, Nutrition Research Institute, Ministry of Health

Einas, Bassim Khaleel, CBI Manager, Ministry of Health

Basima Muhamed Sadiq Al-Sahibi, Human Development Office, MOPDC

Household Survey (IHSES) and Strategies for Poverty Reduction (PRS) Project Management Team

Zaki Abdul Wahab Al-Jadir, Project Manager

Abdullah Hasan Mathi, Deputy Project Manager

Qassim E. Frez, Financial Officer

Ahmed M. Saleh, Procurement Officer

Adil Rashid Al-Shemmeri, Logistics Officer

Ghassan Adnan Mahmoud, Follow-Up Officer

Lamyaa A. Razak, Project Accountant

IHSES Data Analysis Team

Dr. Mehdi Muhsin Ismail Al-Alak, Deputy Minister, MOPDC; Head, COSIT
Najla' Ali Murad, Director, Living Conditions Statistics Department
Hana A. Saleh, IHSES, Economic expert
Iman Hassoon Hadi, Data Manager
Ayad Jawad Hasan, Manager of Statistical Analysis Unit
Fadhil Nawgh Khaizaran, Expenditure Indicators
Basma Abdul Wahab Qadoori, Education and Demographic Indicators
Dalia Abdul Latif Abdul Qadir, Income Indicators
Nada Ahmed Amin, Housing Indicators
Sundus Jawad Hussein, Workforce and Ration Card Indicators
Bushra Nsaif Jasim, Health and Loan Indicators
Feryal Mahmoud Kadhim, Time Use Indicators
Mudhafer T. Pirdawood, Demographic Indicators, Erbil
Omed Baker Ahmed, Income Indicators, Sulaimaniya

The World Bank Team

Ritva Reinikka, MENA Sector Director
Hedi Larbi, Middle East Country Director
Farrukh Iqbal, MENA Sector Manager
Susan Razzaz, Task Team Leader

Poverty analysis team

Nicola Amendola, Economist
Sheldon Annis, Technical Writer
Mohammed Bakir, Statistician
Basil Hussaini, Economist
Susan Razzaz, Senior Economist
Marina Sorrentino, Economist
Giovanni Vecchi, Economist,

Technical and administrative support

Dalia Baghdadi, Administrative support
Maria Edo, Research Assistant
Sharon Hainsfurther, Team Coach
Muna Salim, Senior Program Assistant
Ron Weber, Editor

Peer review committee

Gero Carletto, Senior Economist
Louise Cord, Sector Manager
Ishac Diwan, Country Director
Elena Glinskaya, Country Sector Coordinator
Sergei Shatalov, Country Manager

Readers and advisors

Randa Akeel, Economist
Ghassan Al Khoija, Senior Operations Officer
Jorge Araujo, Iraq Lead Country Economist
Jean Jacques Frere, Senior Health Specialist
Jane Sansbury, Senior Operations Officer
Colin Scott, Lead Specialist

Financial Support

The World Bank Iraq Trust Fund (ITF) is a multilateral initiative that was launched in early 2004 to help donor nations channel and coordinate support for the reconstruction of Iraq. Financial resources for the present work were provided through he Household Survey and Policies for Poverty Reduction (HSPPR) project, which included a US$5.5 million grant executed by the Ministry of Planning and Development Cooperation of Iraq, and a US$3.6 million technical assistance grant executed by the World Bank. International donors to the ITF include the governments of Australia, Canada, the European Community, Finland, Iceland, India, Japan, the Republic of Korea, Kuwait, the Netherlands, Norway, Qatar, Spain, Sweden, Turkey, the United Kingdom, and the United States.

Abbreviations

AKR	average number of calories per person per day
CAP	Consolidated Appeals Process
COSIT	Central Organization for Statistics and Information Technology
CPI	consumer price index
CBN	cost-of-basic-needs (method)
DPT	diphtheria-pertussis-tetanus (vaccine)
GDP	gross domestic product
GOI	Governnment of the Republic of Iraq
HSPPR	Household Survey and Policies for Poverty Reduction
ID	Iraqi dinars
IDP	internally displaced person
IFHS	Iraq Family Health Survey
IHSES	Iraq Household Socio-Economic Survey
ILO	International Labour Organization
IOM	International Organization for Migration
ITF	Iraq Trust Fund
KRG	Kurdistan Regional Government
KRSO	Kurdistan Region Statistics Organization
LMI	lower middle income (country)
LPG	liquefied petroleum gas
MENA	Middle East and North Africa (Region)
MICS	Multiple Indicator Cluster Survey
MOF	Ministry of Finance
MOLSA	Ministry of Labor and Social Affairs
MOPDC	Ministry of Planning and Development Cooperation
PCE	per capita expenditure
PDS	Public Distribution System
PRS	Poverty Reduction Strategy
PRSHC	Poverty Reduction Strategy High Committee
PSU	primary sampling unit
SPN	Social Protection Net (MOLSA)

UNESCO	United Nations Educational, Scientific, and Cultural Organization
UNFPA	United Nations Population Fund
UNHCR	United Nations High Commissioner for Refugees
UNICEF	United Nations Children's Fund
WDI	*World Development Indicators*
WHO	World Health Organization

Executive Summary

This book provides the most comprehensive and rigorous analysis of Iraqi living standards to be carried out in several decades. It makes extensive use of the Iraq Household Socio-Economic Survey (IHSES), the first nationwide income and expenditure survey since 1988. IHSES data were complemented with a wide range of other sources, providing a holistic perspective on living standards that was previously unavailable. The analysis presented here was carried out with two main goals—first, to inform the Government's Poverty Reduction Strategy; and second, to create a baseline against which future progress in poverty reduction can be monitored and assessed.

Iraqi living standards have fallen dramatically over the past generation. Compared with most other countries, there is relatively little inequality in Iraq. This combination—declining living standards, low inequality—is in part a consequence of war and instability; yet even more significantly, it is rooted in decades of neglected social investment. With accumulating deterioration, the economy has generated few jobs, especially in rural areas. Individuals have limited opportunities to benefit from their labor, professional skills, or entrepreneurial activity. Women in particular have been largely excluded from the labor force. School enrollment and life expectancy have both gone down. Poor educational quality and low-productivity jobs have reinforced a vicious cycle: households have little incentive to invest in more schooling, especially among low-income families and for girls in rural areas. Constraints on productivity are further exacerbated by the weaknesses in economic infrastructure outside the oil sector, including lack of access to reliable electricity and water, and even to paved roads.

Few Iraqis today are well-to-do, and few are extremely poor. The relative absence of absolute poverty largely reflects the Public Distribution System (PDS). Nearly the entire population receives food rations, which provide an average of 85 percent of the minimum average caloric requirement. While PDS food rations have been important as a safety net protecting the poor and the vulnerable, the system is exceptionally expensive, inefficient, and fiscally costly. The PDS has accounted for a far greater share of public expenditure than education and health.

Iraq is moving forward. The challenge requires re-development and recovery of what has been lost, including the stimulus provided by economic opportunity. A transition in policy is needed from provision of minimal food subsistence to long-term investments in human productivity. An environment more conducive to the poor can be created by investments that help citizens to benefit from their own labor and education. This challenge is being concretely addressed in the newly adopted national Poverty Reduction Strategy. That strategy, informed by the present analysis, articulates clear priorities for government spending and detailed programmatic actions.

Chapter 1

Introduction

This study represents the second component of collaboration between the Government of Iraq and the World Bank. Initiated in a virtual information vacuum at the outset of Iraq's reconstruction effort in 2004, its purpose is to (i) collect data on poverty and living standards, (ii) analyze the causes, consequences, and characteristics of poverty in Iraq, and (iii) develop a strategy to reduce poverty, generate employment, and improve safety nets. The present study serves as a backdrop to an evolving national discussion on poverty reduction strategies.

The collaboration has been spearheaded by the Poverty Reduction Strategy High Committee (PRSHC), a high-level technical commission convened in 2006 by the Minister of Planning and Development Cooperation, Dr. Barham Salih. PRSHC represents Iraq's parliament, its key development-related ministries (including those of the Kurdistan Region), and the academic community.

For contributors and acknowledgments
Annex 1.1

The primary source of data is the Iraq Household Socio-Economic Survey (IHSES), a yearlong field survey carried out by the Central Organization for Statistics and Information Technology (COSIT) of Iraq and the Kurdistan Region Statistics Organization (KRSO). These data have also been used to update Iraq's consumer price index (CPI) and its national accounts.

Analysis contained in this study was conducted by several partners—PRSHC, the data analysis units of COSIT and KRSO, and the World Bank team. Two particularly important conceptual steps were, first, selection of an appropriate quantitative welfare indicator and, second, setting a poverty line based on the needs and consumption patterns of the Iraqi population and on prevailing prices. The poverty line that was devised for this purpose was subsequently adopted by the Council of Ministers in May 2009.

Building upon the present foundation, PRSHC developed the first National Strategy for Poverty Reduction, including policy priorities and details for public investments. A diverse group of 120 individuals, representing Iraqi stakeholders and the international community, provided a first round of feedback in mid 2009. Follow-up discussions were held with members of the Iraqi Council of Ministers and with key parliamentary committees. The proposed strategy was adopted by the Council of Ministers at a session chaired by Prime Minister Nouri Al-Malki on November 24, 2009. The strategy was formally launched on January 14, 2010, and debated in the Council of Representatives on January 19, 2010.

This book summarizes the main findings from the analytical process. While methodological issues and statistical details are important in this story, for the most part they have been relegated to a supplementary reference volume. Boxes appearing in the margins of pages that follow point readers to corresponding background materials and supplementary statistics. In addition to providing analytic documentation, the reference volume has an important secondary purpose—to assist Iraqi agencies and the international community in prioritizing investments in infrastructure and government services. The disaggregation of data by geographic area, poverty status, gender, and so forth will help to identify particular needs and differences that cannot be fully treated in the summary text.[1]

The following chapter briefly explains the process whereby data were obtained and subsequently analyzed. Thematic chapters then address a series of related questions:

- How big is the problem? How many poor Iraqis are there, and how poor are they? How do their living standards compare to those of neighboring countries, and to the Iraq of past decades? How does inequality in Iraq compare to other countries? (Chapter 3)

- Geographically, *where* are the poor to be found? How does poverty differ among subpopulations, and what are the implications for targeting remedies? To what extent are urban and rural populations different? Are there differences for the Kurdistan Region and the rest of Iraq? How has recent displacement affected the distribution of population and poverty? (Chapter 4)

---

[1] A significant amount of *unanalyzed* data has already been published in the three-volume IHSES Tabulation Report (2008). Volume 1 of the Tabulation Report consists of a description of the field survey and a brief summary of data highlights. Volume 2 consists of several hundred cross-tabulation tables. Volume 3 provides the full IHSES questionnaire, training manual, definitions, and supervisory forms. The IHSES Tabulation Report, as well as the present document, can be downloaded in Arabic (www.cosit.gov.iq) and in English (www.worldbank.or/iq). Readers are cautioned, however, that price data in the Tabulation Report have not been adjusted for inflation or regional variation (see Chapter 2), and thus should be used with extreme caution.

- What is the employment situation in Iraq? Who is employed? Who is unemployed? Who is completely outside the labor force? What kinds of jobs does the economy generate, and does the work of the poor differ from that of the nonpoor? What is the status of agriculture, the main source of livelihood for the rural population? (Chapter 5)

- What are the trends in literacy and school enrollment? To what extent is education rewarded, and can it serve as a pathway out of poverty? If parents are not sending their children to school, why not? (Chapter 6)

- What are the trends in health and physical well-being, and what accounts for them? Are public health services accessible and do the poor make use of them? What is the link between fertility and poverty? (Chapter 7)

- What are living conditions within homes and neighborhoods, for the poor and nonpoor? How accessible and reliable are electricity, clean water, and sanitary facilities? What is the condition of the roads? What about waste collection and neighborhood security? (Chapter 8)

- How well do Iraq's two major social safety nets work—that is, food rations through the Public Distribution System (PDS) and targeted cash transfers through the social protection net (SPN)? If public transfers were to be reformed, what would be the impact? What other kinds of transfers exist and what is their scope? (Chapter 9)

Chapter 10 summarizes key findings and outlines the links between the present analysis and the Poverty Reduction Strategy.

Chapter 2

Collecting Data and Measuring Poverty

The Need for Information

Absence of credible data for economic planning was one among many hurdles that Iraq faced as it began its reconstruction in the wake of regime change in 2003. Political and economic isolation in the 1990s and early 2000s had marginalized Iraq from the explosive growth in information technologies and rapid advances in survey and analytical methods realized in other places. No comprehensive socioeconomic survey had been conducted for nearly 20 years in Iraq. In the interim, existing data had been used selectively and distorted, not only by the previous regime but by outside observers, journalists, and virtually anyone with a political agenda. This situation was badly exacerbated by the turmoil following invasion. Key ministries were already depleted by years of budgetary neglect and the continuous drain of qualified staff. Physical facilities and equipment were then damaged or destroyed. Key records were lost, including much of the existing socioeconomic data that had previously been housed at the Central Statistical Office in Baghdad.

The World Bank reengaged with Iraq in the summer of 2003 in response to international donor requests to help channel resources and coordinate reconstruction. The World Bank Iraq Trust Fund (ITF) was set up in early 2004 with financial support from 17 donor countries. In July 2006, the Bank and the Ministry of Planning and Development Cooperation (MODPC) signed a project agreement to build capacity for evidence-based policy making—in particular, in the area of poverty analysis. The Household Survey and Policies for Poverty Reduction (HSPPR) project provided US$5.1 million to the government to (*a*) conduct the Iraq Household Socio-Economic Survey (IHSES), (b) analyze the data, and (c) develop a poverty reduction strategy. US$1.5 million was included for additional capacity building and technical assistance associated with the survey, data analysis, and strategy development. Based on positive results during the initial effort, US$2.5 million was added in May 2008 so that the project could be scaled up.

Collecting Data: The Iraq Household Socio-Economic Survey

The Iraq Household Socio-Economic Survey, which was carried out under HSPPR, represents the broadest and most systematic household survey ever undertaken in Iraq. The 13-month survey was in the field between October 2006 and November 2007. The lead implementing agencies were the Iraq Central Organization for Statistics and Information Technology (COSIT) and the Kurdistan Region Statistical Organization (KRSO).

Data were collected from a probability-based sample representing the entire national population. Each of Iraq's 18 governorates was covered. The IHSES data set is unique not only in that it represents the entire national population, but in its range of subject matter and its level of detail. The combination of representativeness, broad content, and quantitative detail allow depth of analysis into the causes and consequences of poverty that goes beyond typical household surveys. In addition, the database provided specific inputs that were needed to update national accounts and the consumer price index (CPI) of Iraq.

The IHSES questionnaire

The IHSES questionnaire was based on a household questionnaire that was initially developed by the Central Statistical Organization in 2002, and then expanded to include a broader range of living standard measures. Extensive training materials and a field manual were developed in tandem. The 356-item questionnaire was revised through multiple iterations and finalized in March 2006 following pretesting and a pilot survey conducted among 216 households.

The complete IHSES questionnaire and the accompanying training manual, see *IHSES Tabulation Report, Volume 3* (2008).

Part 1 of the questionnaire covers socio-demographic characteristics of the population. These include the makeup of households; receipt and consumption of food rations from the Public Distribution System (PDS); literacy and schooling; illness, injury, and utilization of health services; languages spoken; characteristics of dwellings; absences from the household; job searching and past employment.

Part 2 covers monthly, quarterly, and annual expenditures (food as well as nonfood spending). The information is based on recall. Spending on education, health, housing, and other categories was also recorded.

Part 3 includes detailed questions on types of work performed by each member of the household; income from wage and nonwage work (including microenterprise and household agricultural production); income from property and transfers; ownership of durable goods; loans received; and risks faced by the household, including direct impacts of the security situation such as threats, material losses, and human casualties.

Part 4 provides a diary for recording daily expenditures on food and other frequently purchased goods and services. Households were provided with a daily ledger in which to track precise costs and quantities. Interviewers were trained to assist respondents in accurate measurement and recording.

Finally, a detailed time-use sheet was included. This covers all activities for every member of the household 10 years or older. The time-use questionnaire covers a random subsample of one-third of all households interviewed.

The sample

The population covered by IHSES included all households residing in Iraq between November 1, 2006, and October 30, 2007—meaning that every Iraqi household within Iraq's geographical boundaries had an equal chance of being included.

Selecting the sample and merging databases, Annex 2.1

The 1997 population census served as the sample frame for the 15 governorates that participated in that census.[2] The sample was designed to permit analysis at the level of 56 strata, defined as the rural areas, urban areas, and governorate centers of each of Iraq's 18 governorates. (Baghdad Governorate was the exception, with five rather than three strata.)

IHSES organization and fieldwork management, Annex 2.2

The sample was selected in two stages. First, 54 sample points were selected from among the primary sampling units (PSUs) within each stratum. Each of the 3,024 sample points was then mapped and listed to reflect population changes since

---

[2] For Erbil and Duhouk, the enumeration frame from the 2004 Living Condition Survey was updated and used. For Sulaimaniya, the enumeration frame from the compulsory education project was used.

the 1997 census. Second, a cluster of six households was selected from each sample point. The total sample was thus composed of six households in each of 3,024 sample points, for a nominal sample of 18,144 households. Of these, 17,822 households were actually reached. With an average of about 6.9 individuals per household, this translated into a sample of 127,189 individuals. The nominal sample of IHSES was coordinated with the samples of the Iraq Multiple Indicator Cluster Survey 2006 (MICS 2006)[3] and the Iraq Family Health Survey (IFHS). This allowed the data sets to be merged.

Organization of fieldwork

Fieldwork was designed to maximize data quality. IHSES fieldworkers received 23 days of intense training, beginning with theory in the classroom but rapidly transitioning to hands-on practice in the field. The fieldworkers were organized into 56 teams, each comprised of three interviewers, a local supervisor, and a data entry operator. Governorate and regional supervisors worked on the ground along with the constantly moving local teams. The operational structure was decentralized, creating flexibility so that the field teams could adjust to the unpredictability of the rapidly changing security situation. Data entry was similarly decentralized. Automated quality control procedures spotted anomalies and flagged potential errors. With immediate communication between the data managers in Baghdad and local teams still in the field, households could be revisited, repeatedly if necessary, to ensure that data for each household was accurate, usable, and complete.[4] As soon as interviews were completed, files were uploaded to the central server so preliminary analysis could be conducted even before fieldwork was complete.

Exceptional circumstances

When households could not be reached,
Annex 2.4

The period of October–November 2006 (that is, the first two months of IHSES fieldwork) took place during the peak of Iraq's recent civil violence—nearly 3,000 confirmed casualties per month according to Iraq Body Count statistics. In many areas of Baghdad,

---

[3] The Iraq Multiple Indicator Cluster Survey 2006 (MICS 2006) was carried out by the Central Organization for Statistics and Information Technology and the Kurdistan Region Statistics Office in collaboration with the Ministry of Health. Financial and technical support was provided by the United Nations Children's Fund (UNICEF). MICS 2006 was conducted during the third round of MICS surveys carried out in more than 50 countries in 2005 and 2006.

[4] A minimum of seven visits was made to each household to complete all five parts of the questionnaire and to assist with the diary of expenditures. An additional visit was made afterward if there were any remaining anomalies or potential errors in the data.

Al-Anbar, Diala, and Salahuddin, government offices had to be closed; markets were regularly shut down; and kidnappings, bombings, and terrorist attacks occurred daily.

Terms such as "difficult situation" and "need for innovative methods" hardly do justice to the "accommodation" (and personal heroism) that was routinely required of IHSES field teams. Interviewers and supervisors had to be hired

Images from the Field, Annex 2.3

locally and be capable of navigating through unpredictable circumstances and pervasive suspicion about the motives and identities of *any* outsiders. Since Iraqi names frequently signal ethnic or tribal affiliation, many interviewers were detained and threatened. In some instances, multiple identity cards had to be issued (for example, omitting a middle name that indicated the interviewer's ethnic or sectarian background) so that interviewers could move from one neighborhood to the next ("a separate identity card in each sock," as one interviewer recently recalled). Fieldworkers frequently opted for old rental cars rather than government vehicles, or they arranged taxi transportation so that they would be accompanied by a well-known local driver. In some areas, regional coordinators converted their homes to makeshift offices, thus avoiding the risks of frequent travel to government offices. In situations where active violence flatly precluded interviewing—a siege in Al-Anbar, for example—interviewers waited out events locally, and then moved on to continue interviews as soon as the siege was lifted. (They then worked longer hours to make up for lost time).

Sometimes a team could not visit a cluster at the scheduled time because of unsafe security conditions. When this happened, that cluster was swapped with a randomly selected cluster scheduled for a later date. If none were considered secure, a sample point was randomly selected from among those that had been visited already, and a new group of six households (randomly selected) was visited. Remarkably few of the original clusters could not be visited during the fieldwork. Nationally, fewer than 2 percent of the original clusters (55 of 3,024) had to be replaced.

Measuring Poverty

Selection and construction
 of a welfare indicator,
Annex 2.5.

Poverty analysis requires three things: first, an empirical indicator to measure living standards; second, a threshold value (referred to as the poverty line) that distinguishes poor from nonpoor; and third, a set of indices that describe poverty in the population. The field of economics has produced no shortage of methodological options and debate on how to interpret and measure these three elements. Each alternative has respective advantages and drawbacks. The Poverty Reduction Strategy High Committee assessed these alternatives and adopted the following approach, which was endorsed by the Iraqi Council of Ministers and is used throughout this report.

An empirical indicator to measure the living standard

One difficulty associated with choosing a measurable indicator is that the concept of living standard is intrinsically multidimensional. The approach that was adopted here is sometimes referred to as the "welfarist approach." It is based upon the notion that individuals are best able to judge their own needs and that they express their needs through their expenditures on consumption. Measuring consumption therefore serves to reveal individual preference, utility, and consequently welfare level. This may be a theoretical argument, but it is well supported by observation and a great deal of empirical testing.[5] International best practice generally endorses the notion that a comprehensive measure of consumption has tremendous explanatory power when applied to measurement of living standards.[6]

---

[5] See, for example, P. Lanjouw, "Constructing a Consumption Aggregate for the Purpose of Welfare Analysis: Principles, Issues, and Recommendations Arising from the Case of Brazil." World Bank, Washington, DC, February 2009.

[6] There are three advantages to consumption over income as a measure of living standards. First, consumption is fairly comprehensive. Second, consumption data tends to be more reliable than income data due to incomplete measurement or frequent underreporting of income. Third, consumption expenditures tend to fluctuate less than income (which can even go to zero in certain months due to seasonal factors), making consumption a more appropriate indicator of *permanent* (or average) living standard.

The measure of living standard that is used throughout this paper is referred to as per capita expenditure (PCE). PCE is defined as the ratio between nominal household expenditure[7] and the product of three factors required to adjust for variations in household needs and purchasing power (household size, temporal CPI, and spatial CPI).[8] That is to say,

Constructing consumer
price indexes (CPIs),
Annex 2.6

$$PCE = \frac{\text{Nominal household consumption expenditure}}{\text{Household size x Temporal CPI x Spatial CPI}}$$

Of course, some relevant aspects of well-being are not captured by a single monetary welfare measure such as PCE. Accordingly, this document supplements poverty measures based on PCE with other kinds of nonmonetary indicators—for example, indicators that describe education, health, or characteristics of the physical living environment.

A threshold value (poverty line) to separate poor from nonpoor

An approach known as the cost-of-basic-needs (CBN) method was used to categorize households as poor versus nonpoor. The CBN method defines the poverty line as the level of expenditure that allows a household to spend just enough on *food* to afford the cost of a minimum required energy intake, and just enough to

---

[7] Nominal household consumption expenditure includes food, housing, services, and other consumption expenditures. Two points are particularly important to keep in mind. First, a large part of Iraqi food consumption is acquired as PDS food rations at below market prices. It is necessary to combine consumption of food rations with consumption of food purchased at market prices. Second, the vast majority of Iraqis (both poor and nonpoor) live in homes they own rather than rent. To compare housing consumption (namely, the stream of services provided by housing) between owners and renters, owner-occupied housing was evaluated using imputed rents. The construction of the per capita expenditure variable, including the details of nominal household consumption expenditure, is explained in Annex 2.5.

[8] Because prices vary significantly over time and across different parts of the country, the purchasing power (hence living standards) associated with each dinar spent will vary as well. To compare the living standards of various households, two kinds of adjustments were needed—first, adjustments for variations in prices over time (inflation, which is referred to as the temporal CPI); and second, variations in prices in different parts of the country (the spatial CPI). Both types of purchasing power adjustments are described in detail in Annex 2.6.

meet basic *nonfood* needs. The total poverty line (Z) represents the two taken together—in other words, the sum of a food poverty line (Z_F) plus an allowance for nonfood consumption (Z_{NF}).

$$Z = Z_F + Z_{NF}$$

$$Z = (\text{AKR} * \text{cost per calorie}) + E[x_{\text{nonfood}} | x_{\text{food}} \cong Z_F]$$

Setting a poverty line, the CBN method, Annex 2.7

The food poverty line (Z_F) is defined as the average number of calories per person per day (AKR) required to meet energy requirements multiplied by the cost per calorie. The *AKR* that is used here is Iraq-specific. It was calculated based on information on the composition of the Iraqi population by age and gender; the average body weight of Iraqis by age and gender; and average level of physical activity by age, gender, and geographic location.[9] (Adjustments were also made for the special caloric needs of pregnant and breast-feeding women.)

Following this methodology, AKR for the average Iraqi was calculated at 2,337 calories per person per day.[10] Cost per calorie was calculated by dividing total expenditure on food by the total caloric intake for each household in the sample. Poorer households generally consume less-expensive food than richer households and therefore spend less per calorie, so a reference group—the the second and third PCE deciles—was chosen to establish a reasonable cost per calorie. Based on the reference group expenditure, the cost of one calorie was calculated at ID 0.4817.[11] Multiplying this amount by the AKR, the food poverty line (Z_F) was thus set at ID 34,249 per person per month.

---

[9] Urban Iraqis are assumed to have "active or moderately active lifestyles," while rural Iraqis are attributed "vigorous or vigorously active lifestyles."

[10] The average AKR used in poverty analysis among eight MENA countries is 2,193.

[11] Note that more than two-thirds of caloric intake comes from the PDS food ration rather than food purchased at market prices. To combine various caloric sources of calories, all food costs were translated into market prices. Thus the estimated cost per calorie that was used for analytical purposes is higher than the cost that Iraqi households actually paid.

Calculating a reasonable allowance for the second component of poverty line expenditure—*non*food basic needs—is more difficult because the required consumption of shelter, education, and health services varies so widely across contexts. This difficulty was addressed using a methodology proposed by Ravallion.[12] A group of households was identified whose food expenditure is approximately equal to the food poverty line.[13] It was assumed that the nonfood expenditure of this group would also serve as a reasonable approximation of nonfood expenditure at the poverty line. Based on this assumption, the nonfood allowance was then calculated at ID 42,647 per person per month.

Combining the amount calculated for the food poverty line (Z_F equals ID 34,249 person/month) with the amount calculated for nonfood allowance (Z_{NF} equals ID 42,647 person/month), the poverty line for Iraq thus becomes ID 76,896 per person per month.

In other words, any Iraqi living in a household with monthly per capita expenditure *lower* than ID 76,896 is classified as poor. Any Iraqi living in a household with monthly per capita expenditure *greater* than ID 76,896 is classified as nonpoor. That distinction defines poor versus nonpoor throughout this analysis.

A set of indices to describe poverty

With measurement of a living standard and a way to distinguish poor from nonpoor, it also becomes possible to identify who is poor within the population and how poor they are. Programmatically, the poor can then be targeted, and progress tracked toward concrete goals. Analytically, the characteristics and correlates of poverty can then be dissected, allowing for exploration of the underlying causes of poverty.

This is the stage where the third ingredient of poverty analysis comes into play, namely a set of poverty measures. Within both the scholarly literature and among practitioners around the world, the most common tools are a family of indicators

---

[12] Among many papers, see for example, M. Ravallion, *Poverty Comparisons* (Fundamentals of Pure and Applied Economics 56). Chur, Switzerland; Langhorne, PA: Harwood Academic Press, 1994.

[13] Details of the calculations are provided in Annex 2.7. The most commonly used approach for calculating the nonfood allowance (also suggested by Ravallion, 1994) is based on the behavior of those whose total expenditures are approximately equal to the food poverty line. This approach was deemed inappropriate for Iraq, where only 0.5 percent of the population have total expenditures lower than the food poverty line, thanks to the existence of the Public Distribution System (food ration).

that was first suggested by Foster, Greer, and Thorbecke.[14] These indices are used to describe the extent of poverty (usually a headcount ratio expressed as a percentage); the intensity of poverty (measured as the poverty gap, or the poverty gap squared); and inequality (most commonly the Gini coefficient).

A summary of these indices for Iraq, based on IHSES data, is presented at the outset of the following chapter, and the overall picture that they paint is then briefly described. Subsequent chapters consider the poverty data in terms of particular themes such as income, education, and health. The final chapter joins the programmatic and analytic perspectives by considering the official National Strategy for Poverty Reduction (adopted in November 2009) in light of the foregoing analytic discussion.

---

[14] J. Foster, J. Greer, and E. Thorbecke, 1984, "A Class of Decomposable Poverty Measures," *Econometrica* 52 (3): 761–66.

Chapter 3

Living Standards, Inequality, and Poverty

Summary of Basic Indicators

Understanding living standards, inequality, and poverty in Iraq begins with the basic indicators that are summarized in Table 3.1. Several key points stand out:

- Iraqi GDP fell from US$3,375 in 1980 to US$1,665 in 2006.

- Inequality in living standards is extremely low in Iraq. The Gini coefficient, the most commonly used measured of inequality, is only .309

- Of Iraq's 30+ million population, approximately 6.9 million are classified as poor. Of the total poor population, about half (3.44 million) live in rural areas and half (3.45 million) live in urban areas.

- Expressed as a share, between a fifth and a quarter (22.9 percent) of the population is poor.[15] In rural areas, the poverty rate is 39.3 percent, more than twice the 16.1 percent rate in urban areas.

- Iraq's poverty gap index (4.5 percent) is extremely low compared to that of most other countries. The poverty gap index for the rural population (9.0 percent) is more than three times higher than for the urban population (2.7 percent). This implies that not only a higher share of rural population that is poor, but also that the rural population is relatively poorer.

- The severity of poverty as measured by the poverty gap index squared (1.4 percent) is also extremely low.[16]

---

[15] The phrase "between a fifth and a quarter" reflects the lower (20.9 percent) and upper (24.8 percent) bounds of the 95 percent confidence interval for the point estimate of 22.9 percent.

[16] A shift in expenditure from a person below the poverty line to an even poorer person does not change the poverty gap index. It does, however, change the poverty gap squared. For this reason, the poverty gap squared is of practical importance to policy makers. It makes extreme poverty "visible" in a programmatic sense—for example, for programs that prioritize spending on the poorest of the poor.

Table 3.1 Summary of Key Poverty Indicators

GDP per capita (current US dollars): US$3,375 (1980); US$1,665 (2006)
Gini coefficient (2007): .309

	Total	Rural	Urban
Population of poor (millions)			
The *number* of Iraqis below the official poverty line.	6.89	3.44	3.45
Poverty headcount index (%)			
The *share* of the population below the official poverty line.	22.9	39.3	16.1
Poverty gap index (%)	4.5	9.0	2.7
The *depth* of poverty—that is, the average gap between poor people's living standard (their per capita expenditure) and the poverty line. The poverty gap is expressed as a percentage of the poverty line. (Note: Poverty headcount conveys *how many*; poverty gap conveys *how poor*.)			
Poverty-gap-squared index (%)	1.4	3.1	0.7
The *severity* of poverty—that is, inequality among the poor, expressed as a percentage of the poverty line. The average of the square of the gap between poor people's living standards (their per capita expenditure) and the poverty line.			
Aggregate poverty deficit (ID billions/year)	1,261	728	533
The amount of resources that would, in principle, bring every poor person's per capita expenditure exactly up to the poverty line—in other words, the amount of resources needed to fill the poverty gap (assuming that resources could be perfectly targeted in this way).			
Poverty headcount index, using US$2.50 per day standard (%)	13.9	25.9	9.0
A poverty line set in purchasing power parity (PPP) terms to facilitate comparison among countries. The World Bank frequently uses the US$2.50-a-day standard to compare middle- and lower-middle-income countries.[a]			

a. The World Bank uses several standards denominated in U.S. dollars to compare poverty rates among countries, including US$1, US$1.25, and US$2 a day. Much has been written on the pros and cons of various rates.

- The amount of resources that would, in principle, bring every poor person exactly up to the poverty line—in principle filling the poverty gap—would be just US$1.3 billion per year. This amount should not be interpreted as the budgetary cost to eliminate poverty.[17] Nevertheless, it is interesting to contemplate (if only as a thought exercise) that the total aggregate poverty deficit would be equivalent to less than 2 percent of Iraq's 2008 budget of US$72 billion.

- Iraq's headcount index of 22.9 percent (based on the Iraqi poverty line of ID 76,896 per person per month) is substantially higher than the headcount index of 13.9 percent (based on the international poverty line of US$2.50 per person per day). The international poverty line is a convenient tool often used to make comparisons among countries.[18] However, Iraq's official poverty line of ID 76,896 per person per month—based on actual needs and consumption of the Iraqi population—is far more useful for analysis of the causes and consequences of poverty within Iraq.

Understanding Living Standards, Inequality, and Poverty

Although Iraq contains many poor people, the country itself is not poor— neither in its natural resources or historically. Rather, Iraq is a middle-income country whose standard of living has declined over the past 25 years. Figure 3.1 shows that gross domestic product (GDP) per person declined by fully a third between 1980 and 2006—from about US$3,000 to about US$2,000. What is striking, however, is not just the decline, but also that reversal in growth stands in contrast to every other country in the Middle East and North Africa (MENA) region.

Social trends have paralleled economic trends over the past 25 years. Figure 3.2 illustrates primary school enrollment, an area in which Iraq once led the region. As with GDP per capita, primary enrollments declined over the past 25 years in Iraq while rising in every other MENA country.

---

[17] In point of fact, perfect targeting is never possible. Similarly, the hypothetical amount represented by the aggregate poverty deficit does not include costs to manage this expenditure if it were conceived as an actual transfer program. Moreover, as the National Poverty Reduction Strategy makes clear, transfer programs—while an important part of a poverty reduction strategy—are neither the only nor the best way to reduce poverty. Programs that increase the productivity of the poor are also needed and can have permanent poverty reduction impacts.

[18] Using the same measure, the average MENA headcount is 28.4 percent, and the lower-middle-income (LMI) country average is 43.1 percent. See http://iresearch.worldbank.org /PovcalNet/povcalNet.html.

Figure 3.1. GDP per Capita in MENA Countries, 1980–2006

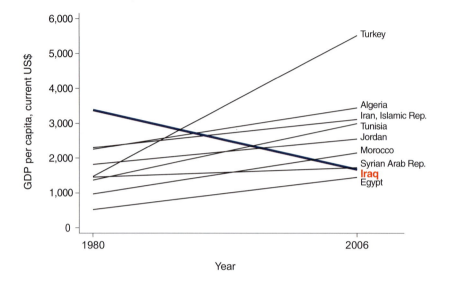

Figure 3.2. Primary School Enrollment in MENA Countries, 1980-2006

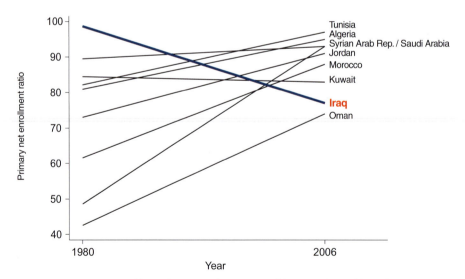

Sources: For 2006, *World Development Indicators.* Washington, DC: World Bank, 2008: CD version; for 1980, UNESCO Institute for Statistics, Data Center, online database.

From the point of view of strategic planning, *re*development poses quite a different problem than development for the first time. Both conceptually and practically, poverty in a country that has declined is not the same as poverty in a country that historically has been poor.

The scattergram in Figure 3.3 illustrates Iraq's inequality within a global comparative perspective. The 127 dots represent countries plotted according to their level of inequality (vertical axis) and their GDP per capita (horizontal axis). The downward-sloping line represents the overall negative correlation between GDP per capita and inequality. Iraq is an outlier identified in red in the lower left corner. In brief: No country at Iraq's level of per capita GDP has a lower level of inequality; and virtually all countries at Iraq's level of GDP per capita have higher levels of inequality.[19]

Figure 3.3. Inequality (Gini Index) and GDP per Capita for 127 Countries

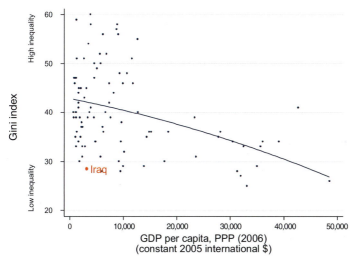

Source: World Development Indicators (2008: CD version); IHSES for Iraq

---

[19] Annex 3.1 provides additional perspective on comparative inequality. For example, Figure 3.1-1 in the annex shows Iraq's Gini coefficient (.309) to be far lower than comparator countries such as Morocco (.395) or Turkey (.436). (The Gini coefficient of .309 for Iraq is based on expenditures unadjusted for spatial differences in the cost of living within the country. This is consistent with the numbers provided for other countries. The Gini coefficient for Iraq based on spatially *adjusted* expenditures is .285. The Gini coefficient for Iraq based on spatially *unadjusted income* is .359.)

Inequality in regional and
international perspective,
Annex 3.1

How is this to be interpreted? Those countries whose levels of inequality are as low or lower than Iraq's are generally far wealthier per capita, such as Denmark, Japan, Sweden, Iceland, or the Czech Republic. For the most part, these are countries with longstanding traditions of inclusive economic growth and strong public services.

Iraq's position in the figure reflects a different story: During the previous 25 years, Iraq's government largely ignored economic and social investment that might have increased employment and productivity. Instead, the government used untargeted food subsidies to address social needs.[20] While equality is generally considered a good thing, the kind of "equality" that Iraq achieved could more accurately be described as a leveling process. Relative to Iraq's resources, the leveling process did not particularly benefit the vast majority of the population, neither those at the top nor those at the bottom of the distribution.

While the Gini coefficient summarizes the overall level of inequality, it says little about the distribution of living standards or the differences that separate poor from nonpoor. Figure 3.4 depicts the distribution of living standards (measured by per capita expenditure) in relation to the poverty line at ID 76,896 per person per month. The most striking feature of the figure is that the vast majority of the poor are *just* below the poverty line, while the majority of the nonpoor population is *just* above the poverty line.

The characteristics of the distribution curve—that is, the strong skew to the left and the narrow standard deviation around the mean—have important ramifications for welfare analysis. Consider what happens, for example, when the population confronts shocks at either the personal or the macroeconomic level. Personal shocks can be related to circumstances such as death of a wage earner, loss of employment, or unusually high medical expenses due to injury or illness. Macro shocks, which affect nearly everyone across the board, could be related to inflation, devaluation of the national currency, a downturn in a crucial sector, or a security crisis that depresses economic activity overall. Both kinds of shocks are more than common in Iraq.

---

[20] The recent security situation and the legacy of sanctions, too, have depressed economic activity and consumption of luxuries.

Figure 3.4. Population Distribution by per Capita Expenditure

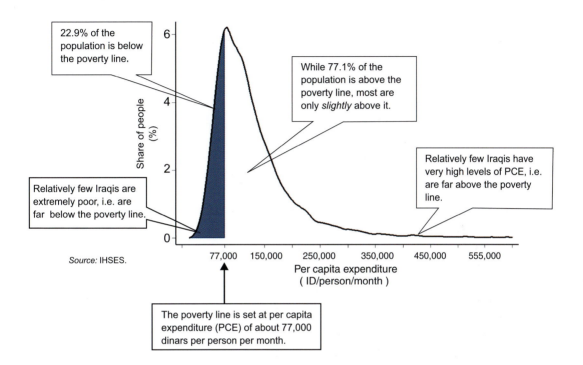

Source: IHSES.

The impact of shocks are different for those at different points on a welfare distribution. Take for example, a shock in the form of an increase in the price of wheat. In a country where almost everyone is well above the poverty line, welfare might decline overall but a large number of people who not be pushed below the poverty line. In Iraq, however—where the majority of the total population is already close to the poverty line—even a moderate increase in food prices could result in a large increase in poverty. In other words, the majority of the Iraqi population is only "one or two shocks" away from poverty.

Shocks, by urban/rural and poverty status, [Annex 3.2](#)

On the other hand, the welfare distribution in Iraq also has a more positive aspect. As indicated by its poverty gap index of 4.1 percent and the poverty gap squared index of 1.9 percent, Iraqi poverty is very shallow. By international standards, a poverty deficit of US$1.3 billion could be considered "good news" in the context of an economy of US$91 billion. It is a scale of poverty that can be realistically addressed,

21

Chapter 4

Geographic Variation
in Poverty

The Geographic Distribution of Poverty in Iraq

Despite an unusually low level of inequality when compared with other countries (Chapter 3), poverty within Iraq is unevenly distributed geographically. This chapter looks at internal variation more closely, starting with the key poverty indicators and the urban-rural divide. The key indicators are broken down geographically in Table 4.1 on the following page. This chapter also considers the relatively lower levels of poverty in the Kurdistan Region of Iraq, as well as and the geographic implications of recent population displacement. Chapter 5, which follows, looks more closely at aricultural productivity, a fundamental source of the urban-rural differences.

Which areas are poorest?

The question of which geographic areas are poorest is not as straightforward as it may seem because, as discussed, there are several ways to measure poverty. Table 4.1 shows the overall population broken down geographically according to the major poverty indicators. The country is divided into 54 areas. These areas correspond to the three strata used for the IHSES survey (governorate center, rural, and other urban) further broken down for each of the 18 governorates. Figure 4.1 is a reference map that shows the 18 governorates and their governorate centers.

Figure 4.1. Iraq: Governorates and Governorate Centers

Source: Map Design Unit, World Bank.

23

Table 4.1. Poverty by Geographic Area, Ranked by Headcount

Rank	Region	Population (000s)	Share total population (%)	Poverty headcount index (%)	Poverty gap index (%)	Poverty gap squared index (%)	Poor population (000s)	Share poor population (% total)	Monthly PCE (avg.) (ID 000)	Monthly PCE among the poor (avg.) (ID 000)
1	Rural Al-Muthanna	325.7	1.1	**74.7**	23.9	9.9	243.3	3.5	64	52
2	Rural Babil	780.7	2.6	**61.3**	14.8	4.9	478.6	7.0	81	58
3	Rural Wasit	366.4	1.2	**60.1**	18.8	7.5	220.2	3.2	78	53
4	Rural Al-Qadisiya	410.1	1.4	**56.3**	13.8	4.5	230.9	3.4	82	58
5	Rural Salahuddin	633.4	2.1	**55.1**	13.8	4.7	349.0	5.1	87	58
6	Rural Thi Qar	642.7	2.1	**45.5**	10.6	3.6	292.4	2.8	85	59
7	Rural Kerbela	239.0	0.8	**42.3**	8.7	2.7	101.1	1.5	92	61
8	Rural Diala	736.9	2.4	**41.4**	9.7	4.1	305.1	4.4	90	59
9	Rural Al-Najaf	332.8	1.1	**40.8**	7.8	2.3	135.8	2.0	92	62
10	Rural Al-Anbar	577.9	1.9	**38.2**	7.5	2.3	220.8	3.2	94	62
11	Gov. center Kerbela	561.9	1.9	**37.6**	6.6	1.4	211.3	3.1	107	63
12	Rural Basrah	469.6	1.6	**35.3**	7.8	2.4	165.8	2.4	96	60
13	Rural Missan	362.5	1.2	**34.0**	5.9	1.5	123.3	1.8	101	63
14	Other urban Babil	396.6	1.3	**33.6**	3.8	0.7	133.3	1.9	107	68
15	Gov. center Basrah	1,035.4	3.4	**32.1**	2.5	0.3	332.4	4.2	116	71
16	Other urban Basrah	903.0	3.0	**30.3**	6.2	1.8	273.6	4.0	101	61
17	Other urban Al-Muthanna	114.4	0.4	**30.1**	5.8	1.7	34.4	0.5	104	62
18	Rural Ninevah	1,252.1	4.2	**28.6**	5.3	1.5	358.1	5.2	102	63
19	Other urban Wasit	383.3	1.3	**25.6**	5.5	1.6	98.1	1.4	113	60
20	Other urban Al-Qadisiya	203.5	0.7	**25.6**	5.7	1.8	52.1	0.8	113	60
21	Other urban Salahuddin	447.0	1.5	**25.0**	4.8	1.4	111.8	1.6	110	62
22	Other urban Thi Qar	543.2	1.8	**24.4**	4.1	1.1	132.5	1.9	114	64
23	Other urban Diala	308.3	1.0	**24.1**	5.9	1.9	74.3	1.1	114	58
24	Other urban Missan	269.0	0.9	**23.3**	2.5	0.5	62.7	0.9	102	69
	Iraq	**30,086**	**100.0**	**22.9**	**4.5**	**1.4**	**6,884**	**100.0**	**127**	**63**
25	Gov. center Thi Qar	501.0	1.7	**22.8**	3.7	0.8	114.2	1.7	119	64
26	Other urban Ninevah	521.7	1.7	**21.8**	4.6	1.4	113.7	1.7	120	61
27	Gov. center Diala	277.8	0.9	**21.0**	2.6	0.6	58.3	0.8	119	67
18	Rural Duhouk	246.1	0.8	**20.5**	3.9	1.2	50.4	0.7	123	62
29	Other Urban Kerbela	101.9	0.3	**20.5**	3.0	0.6	20.9	0.3	121	66
30	Gov. center Al-Najaf	556.5	1.8	**19.8**	3.8	0.9	110.2	1.6	128	62
31	Gov. center Al-Qadisiya	419.4	1.4	**18.8**	3.2	1.0	78.8	1.1	126	64
32	Gov.. center Al- Muthanna	210.0	0.7	**18.6**	2.5	0.6	39.1	0.6	130	66
33	Gov. center Missan	312.5	1.0	**17.0**	2.2	0.4	53.1	0.8	123	67
34	Gov. center Ninevah	1,046.2	3.5	**16.8**	2.9	0.7	175.8	2.6	124	64
35	Gov. center Wasit	302.6	1.0	**16.0**	3.2	1.0	48.4	0.7	134	61
36	Rural Baghdad	503.6	1.7	**14.9**	1.7	0.3	75.0	1.1	126	68
37	Other urban Baghdad	2,336.3	7.8	**14.7**	2.4	0.6	343.4	5.0	112	64
38	Rural Kirkuk	313.9	1.0	**12.5**	1.3	0.2	39.2	0.6	117	69
39	Other urban Kirkuk	75.6	0.3	**12.2**	1.8	0.4	9.2	0.1	123	66
40	Other urban Al-Najaf	223.7	0.7	**11.6**	2.1	0.5	25.9	0.4	141	63
41	Gov. center Baghdad	4,148.0	13.8	**11.5**	2.2	0.6	477.0	6.9	146	62
42	Other urban Al-Anbar	518.0	1.7	**11.4**	1.9	0.5	59.1	0.9	135	64
43	Rural Erbil	259.3	0.9	**10.1**	1.3	0.3	26.2	0.4	145	67
44	Gov. center Babil	396.6	1.3	**9.5**	2.0	0.6	37.7	0.5	145	60
45	Gov. center Kirkuk	739.5	2.5	**8.4**	1.1	0.2	62.1	0.9	144	67
46	Rural Sulaimaniya	302.2	1.0	**7.8**	1.3	0.3	23.6	0.3	158	64
47	Other urban Duhouk	416.2	1.4	**5.9**	1.4	0.5	24.6	0.4	166	58
48	Gov. center Al-Anbar	331.1	1.1	**5.7**	0.8	0.2	18.9	0.3	138	66
49	Other urban Sulaimaniya	645.3	2.1	**3.8**	0.7	0.2	24.5	0.4	211	62
50	Gov. center Duhouk	231.8	0.8	**3.6**	0.3	0.1	8.3	0.1	209	71
51	Other urban Erbil	432.6	1.4	**3.5**	0.6	0.1	15.1	0.2	182	64
52	Gov. center Salahuddin	77.6	0.3	**1.5**	0.2	0.0	1.2	0.0	167	66
53	Gov. center Erbil	717.2	2.4	**0.9**	0.1	0.0	6.4	0.1	239	70
54	Gov. center Sulaimaniya	626.5	2.1	**0.5**	0.0	0.0	3.1	0.1	269	73

Source: IHSES.

Table 4.1 ranks these 54 areas by poverty headcount, the most familiar and intuitive of the poverty indicators (column 5). Poverty headcount represents the percentage of total population in each geographic area whose per capita expenditure (PCE) falls below the poverty line. The five shaded rows at the top of the table show the five areas with the highest rates of poverty. These range from rural Al-Muthanna (75 percent) to rural Salahuddin (about 55 percent). The five shaded rows at the bottom of the table show the five areas with the lowest rates of poverty. These range from the governorate center of Duhouk (4 percent) to the governorate center of Sulaimaniya (0.5 percent).

Figure 4.2 shows the poverty headcount mapped by governorate. The darkly shaded governorates have the highest headcount rates. The lightly shaded governorates have the lowest rates.

In principle, areas with the highest poverty headcount rates do not necessarily have the deepest or most severe poverty. Iraq, however, is notable in that the various measures of poverty are strongly aligned. In other words, areas with the high headcount indices generally have high poverty gap and poverty gap squared indices. This fact has an important policy implication, because it implies that

Figure 4.2. Poverty Headcount by Governorate, 2007

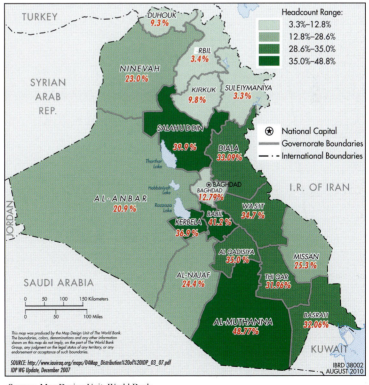

Source: Map Design Unit, World Bank.

25

programs targeting locations with the high rates of poverty (as measured by headcount percentage) are also likely to reach those who are the poorest of the poor (poverty gap and poverty gap squared indices.)

Inequality *within* versus *between* governorates, Annex 4.1

Another striking feature of poverty in Iraq is the strong rural-urban divide. As shown in Table 4.1, the five poorest areas are all rural and five least-poor areas are all urban. On average, 39 percent of rural residents are poor compared to only 16 percent of urban residents. And the rural poor tend to be considerably poorer (poverty gap index of 9 percent rural compared to 2.7 percent urban.)

Figure 4.3 shows the distribution of PCE in rural (red) and urban (blue) areas.[21] The mean rural PCE (ID 97,000, the red dotted vertical line) is itself only about ID 20,000 above the official poverty line indicated by the green arrow. Rural Iraqis are far more likely to have PCE below the poverty line than urban Iraqis. In addition, the rural population is far more homogenous: that is, the rural curve is taller and narrower than the urban curve.

Figure 4.3. Distribution of PCE in Urban and Rural Areas (Percent)

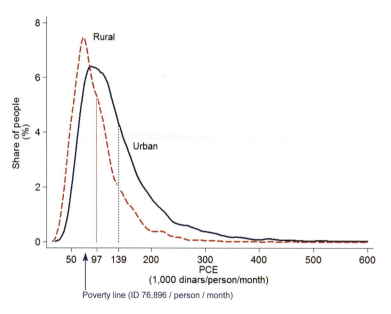

---

[21] For each interval of PCE values, the area below the rural (urban) curve measures the probability that a rural (urban) Iraqi has PCE in that interval.

26

Which areas have the largest numbers of poor people?

The poverty headcount rate, the most familiar and widely used poverty indicator, shows the percentage of population below the poverty line in an area. However, the absolute number of poor people depends upon its population. And as illustrated in the accompanying population density map, the Iraqi population is far from evenly distributed (Figure 4.4).

The population map illustrates that the heaviest concentrations of population (and hence the largest number of poor people) lives in three geographic areas—in and around Baghdad, in the area between Iraq's two great rivers, and in the governorates to the north. While there are important nodes of population elsewhere, the western and southern regions of Iraq are generally sparsely settled. This means that although rural Al-Muthanna has an extremely high poverty headcount (74.7 percent) and the governorate center of Baghdad has a far lower poverty headcount (11.5 percent), about twice as many poor people live in the governorate center of Baghdad than in rural Al-Muthanna. (Nearly 7 percent of all poor Iraqis live in the Baghdad governorate center.)

Figure 4.4. Population Density Map, 2003

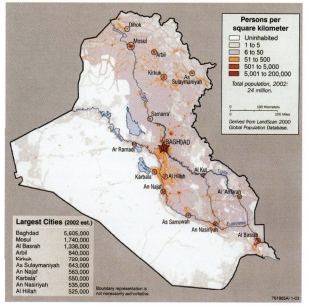

Source: US Government, U-Texas Digital Map Archives, 2003 (public domain map).

Many subtle but important differences emerge when examining the geographic data more closely. The accompanying annexes rank "most to least" from several perspectives:

- Poverty by size of population
- Poverty by size of *poor* population
- The "most" poverty as measured by poverty gap
- Where is poverty most extreme (poverty gap squared)?

Alternative geographic perspectives on poverty, Annex 4.2

27

Differences between the Kurdistan Region and Other Areas

As shown in the preceding discussion, the three governorates of the Kurdistan Region (Duhouk, Erbil, and Sulaimaniya) have notably lower poverty rates than Iraq as a whole. Why?

The differences reflect recent economic and social history. Following its long struggle for autonomy, the Kurdistan Region gained de facto administrative independence in 1991, which was solidified through the creation of the Kurdistan Regional Government (KRG) in 1992. Its geographic position at the crossroads between Turkey, the Islamic Republic of Iran, and the Syrian Arab Republic led to dynamic cross-border trade. In turn, trade and economic competition with its neighbors stimulated higher productivity within the region itself. Thus, while the rest of Iraq was cut off from the outside world after 1991, the Kurdistan Region continued the exchange of goods and knowledge beyond its borders.

The economic situation in the Kurdistan Region improved after 2003 in both absolute and relative terms. Compared with the rest of Iraq, the security situation was relatively stable. IHSES data show, for example, that less than 1 percent of the population of the Kurdistan Region experienced security-related violence (versus 6.6 percent nationally). The business environment was also favorable, including access to credit and a law to attract foreign investment. In personal access to credit, for example, 51 percent of the population had outstanding loans, compared to 38 percent nationally. Similarly, the unemployment rate has stayed at about 6.1 percent in the Kurdistan Region, compared to 11.7 percent nationally.

The Kurdistan Region is different from the rest of Iraq in several aspects that are strongly associated with poverty. For example, a smaller proportion of the population is rural (21 percent compared to 30 percent nationally), and fertility rates are lower (3.8 children per woman compared to 4.3 nationally).

Current school enrollment rates are higher in the Kurdistan Region than in the rest of Iraq. Net primary enrollment is 90 percent compared to 85 percent nationally; net intermediate enrollment is 47 percent compared to 37 percent nationally; and net secondary enrollment is 22 percent compared to 21 percent nationally. These higher rates appear to reflect the region's recent prosperity rather than longstanding historical or cultural differences. Although current enrollment rates are significantly higher in the Kurdistan Region, the reverse was true a generation ago. Among adults, the illiteracy rate in the Kurdistan Region (27 percent) is significantly *higher* than in the rest of the country (19 percent nationally).

Population Displacement

Violence since 2003 forced many Iraqis to flee to safer locations both within and outside of Iraq. The best available evidence suggests that between 2003 and 2009 approximately 1.6 million persons were displaced internally, with at least another million displaced to other countries. Most displacement occurred between 2006 and early 2007, especially after the bombing of Samarra Al-Askari Mosque in February 2006.

As of early 2010, a limited number of people have returned to their homes. According to the United Nations High Commissioner for Refugees (UNHCR), about 426,000 Iraqis returned to their place of origin in 2008 and 2009.[22]

No systematic survey has been carried out on internally displaced persons (IDPs). The quality of existing data is not good because much of the displacement is undocumented, poorly documented, or took place illegally. Only a small portion of refugees in neighboring countries have registered with the United Nations High Commissioner for Refugees.[23]

Figure 4.5 on the following page shows the numbers of IDPs and rates of increase in governorate populations. As shown on the map, the largest share of internal displacement is from Baghdad (nearly two-thirds of all displaced persons according to the International Organization for Migration[IOM]). Although most IDPs have moved within Baghdad itself, significant population shifts have also taken place toward Duhouk, Diala, Kerbela, and Wasit.

The IHSES questionnaire did not directly inquire about or attempt to track internal displacement. However, because of its broad sampling of the population, IHSES was inclusive of many internally displaced persons. Some patterns on displacement can therefore be deduced.

In general, Iraqis tend not to move frequently, and the vast majority own rather than rent their homes (see Chapter 8). By contrast, internally displaced persons generally live in rented housing or with other families (according to IOM in 2009). It is therefore reasonable to infer that a large fraction of IHSES households renting their dwellings and living at their residences for less than two years at the time of the survey (October 2007–November 2007) felt obliged to move due to violence in their areas. IHSES found that approximately 4 percent of households had resided at

---

[22] "Displacement Assessment and Statistics" are available at http://www.iom.int/jahia/Jahia/iraq. This monthly publication also reports that the government of Iraq has stopped registering new internally displaced persons.

[23] According to the United Nations Consolidated Appeal (2009), just over 310,000 refugees had registered with UNHCR by the end of September 2008.

Figure 4.5. Number of Internally Displaced Persons, by Governorate

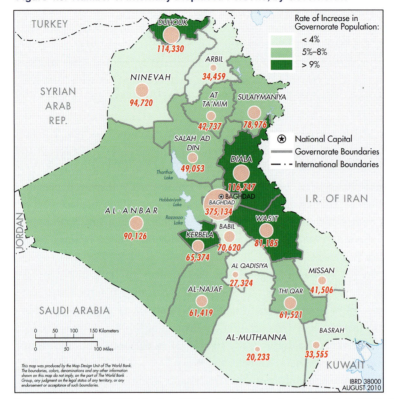

Source: IDP WG Update (2007), taken from UN Inter-Agency Information and Analysis Unit Web site ; rendered by Map DesignUnit, World Bank.

their current dwelling for less than two years, and 7.9 percent between three and five years. Thus the IHSES data appear roughly consistent with the Ministry of Displacement and Migration estimate of 5 percent of the population having been internally displaced since 2006.

Of those who have been in their residence two years or less (many of whom moved due to violence in their areas) 16 percent are poor. This suggests that displaced people are *less likely* to be poor than the average Iraqi. (Recall that on average about 23 percent of Iraqis are poor.) This is reasonable because the poor are more likely to have lived in rural areas where rates of violence were lower.[24]

---

[24] Three percent of the Iraqi population reported kidnapping or security-related violence during the 12 months that preceded their IHSES interview. In general, reports of security related problems are very localized; so the share suffering from kidnapping or violence is high in areas such as Baghdad and Diala, but negligible in other areas. These differences broken down are provided in detail in Annex 2.1 of this report, which shows "shocks" by poverty status and geographic areas.

Moreover, the poor are relatively less likely to have had the resources to move, even those experiencing the same rates of violence.

UNHCR (2007) estimates that perhaps 700,000 Iraqis may now be living in Syria. As shown in Figure 4.6, 600,000–800,000 Iraqis were estimated to have been displaced to Jordan by 2007, with smaller though still significant numbers to the Gulf States, Europe, the Islamic Republic of Iran, the Arab Republic of Egypt, and other countries.[25]

Figure 4.6. Displacement of Iraqis to Neighboring Countries

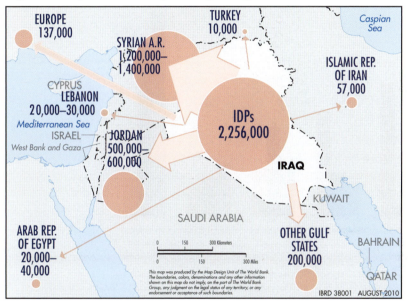

Source: IDP WG Update (2007), taken from UN Inter-Agency Information and Analysis Unit Web site; rendered by Map DesignUnit, World Bank.

There are scant data with which to assess the poverty status of these refugees. Anecdotally at least, it is reasonably evident that Iraqis living in Jordan are generally better off than those living in Syria. It is estimated that about a quarter of Iraqis own their dwellings in Jordan, compared with only 2 percent in Syria, as well as 79 percent who own their own homes in Iraq itself.

---

[25] For more information, see various reports on refugees and displaced persons available from the Consolidated Appeals Process (CAP), 2009; IOM, February 2009; and the Brookings Institution, Washington DC, 2009.

Accurate data are not available on the amount of financial resources that have been lost from Iraq due to massive emigration or the impact this may have had on domestic poverty. Yet in the long run, the loss of human resources may prove even greater and harder to replace than the direct economic loss. Figure 4.7 compares educational attainment of Iraqis living in Jordan, Syria, and in Iraq itself.

Figure 4.7. Educational Attainment of Iraqis Living in Jordan, Syria, and Iraq

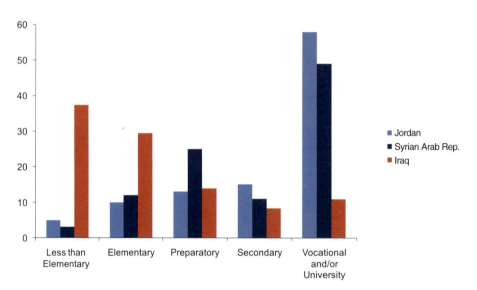

Sources: Iraq—IHSES. *Syria*—IPSOS (survey research firm) and UNHCR. *Jordan*—Fafo (Norwegian Research Institute), the Government of Jordan's Department of Statistics, and the United Nations Population Fund (UNFPA).

It will be noted, first, that Iraqis living in Jordan are substantially better educated than those living in Syria. More striking, however, is the broader contrast between those who left (whether to Syria or Jordan) and those who stayed. Emigration in general was heavily biased toward those who had the means to leave—not only financially, but who were also better educated, more skilled, and better connected in general. This included many business people capable of generating new jobs in the private sector, as well as teachers, health workers, and public administrators capable of enhancing human capacities within a society struggling with reconstruction. The full cost of this loss will be made clearer in the chapters that follow. These look more closely at the relationship between poverty and employment (Chapter 5), education (Chapter 6), and health (Chapter 7).

One of the best ways to understand poverty more finely is to consider the breakdown of expenditure on consumption (PCE) across geographic areas and among groups of people. Annex 4.3 includes about 40 tables that detail this breakdown of expenditure for each of Iraq's governorates.

PCE expenditure by geographic variation and poverty status, Annex 4.3

Chapter 5

Work, Income, and Agriculture

Income from Work and Other Sources

Per capita income is closely tied to poverty at the household level: the more per capita income the household has, the more food, housing, and other goods each individual can consume. Household income comes from three sources. *Employment* income includes wages, the market value of noncash earnings, and cash earnings from self-employment. *Property* income includes investment income as well as the imputed value of owner-occupied housing. *Transfers* include pension income, the market value of food rations and other public transfers, as well as private transfers such as remittances and gifts from other households.

Table 5.1 shows the main components of income. Several observations stand out.

- First, employment accounts for the bulk (about two-thirds) of total household income. Although the nonpoor earn considerably higher absolute amounts, their share of total income from employment is similar for the poor and nonpoor alike.

- Second, the poor earn only 11 percent of their income from property (compared to 19 percent for the nonpoor). Most of the property income of the poor is the imputed value of rent from their owner-occupied homes (see Chapter 9). Many of the nonpoor also own financial or other assets that earn cash income. so include zakat, traditional Islamic "alms for the poor.

Table 5.1. Sources of income by Poverty Status (ID 000/person/month)

Indicator	Non-poor	Poor	Iraq
Employment			
Wages in cash	61.4	38.7	56.2
Wages in kind	1.5	1.4	1.5
Self employment	36.0	19.8	32.3
Total employment	98.9	59.9	90.0
Property[a]			
Imputed rent	24.1	8.6	20.6
Other property	5.2	1.6	4.4
Total property	29.3	10.2	25.0
Transfers[b]			
Pensions	6.2	3.0	5.4
Rations	11.0	11.5	11.1
SSN	0.3	0.2	0.3
Other public in cash	2.0	1.7	1.9
Other public in kind	0.3	0.2	0.3
Private in cash	3.3	1.7	2.9
Private in kind	1.3	0.6	1.1
Total transfers	24.3	18.9	23.1
Total income	152.6	89.0	138.0

Source: IHSES.

Note: Income as used here does not include fuel subsidies or government services for health, education, police, etc.

a. *Income* from ownership of property includes profits, rents received in cash, as well as the value of imputed rent to homeowners. (See Annex 8.1 for methodological explanation of how the imputed value of rent is calculated).
b. *Private transfers* include gifts from other households and remittances from abroad. They also include *zakat*, traditional Islamic "alms for the poor".

Table 5.2. Key Labor Market Indicators

Sources of income
(ID 000/person/month)

	Nonpoor	Poor	Iraq
Employment	99	60	90
Property	29	10	25
Transfers	24	19	23
All sources, total	153	89	138

Age dependency and fertility

	Iraq	MENA	LMI
Share of population < 15 years of age	40%	33%	25%
Age dependency ratio (ADR)	0.7	0.5	0.3
Fertility (births per woman)	4.3	2.9	2.1

Share of population under 15 years of age:

	Poor	Nonpoor
Rural	49%	42%
Urban	45%	36%

Types of work (share of all employed persons)

	All	Poor	Nonpoor
Self-employed in agriculture	15%	29%	11%
Self-employed, not in agriculture	23%	17%	24%
Employee, agriculture	2%	4%	3%
Service employee	53%	42%	56%
Manufacturing employee	7%	8%	6%
Total	100%	100%	100%

Women in the labor force

Women participating in the labor force:

Iraq: 13%   MENA: 30%   LMI: 60%

Share of all working women who work in the education sector: 33%

Share of *poor* working women who work in nonwage agriculture: 75%

Share of *poor, rural* working women who work on wage agriculture: 90%

Economic dependency

Employed persons (including children) as a share of total population:

Iraq: 24%   MENA: 32%   LMI: 50%

Poor rural: 23%   Nonpoor rural: 25%

Poor urban: 19%   Nonpoor urban: 24%

Economic Dependency Ratio (EDR)

Iraq	MENA	LMI
3.2	2.1	0.3

Labor force status of adults

Share of adults (15+ years) who are employed:

	Poor	Nonpoor
Rural	41%	40%
men	67%	67%
women	17%	15%
Urban	33%	38%
men	64%	66%
women	3%	11%

	Employed	Unemployed	Not in labor force
Poor	37%	7%	56%
Nonpoor	38%	5%	57%
All adults	38%	5%	57%
men	66%	9%	25%
women	11%	2%	87%

Share of adults employed:	Iraq	MENA	LMI
	38%	46%	67%

Public sector employment

Shares of all working persons who work in the public sector:

Of all working adults: 32%

Of poor working adults: 17%

Of nonpoor working adults: 36%

Share of highest (PCE) decile workers who work in the public sector: 49%

Sources: IHSES and *World Development Indicators* (2008: CD version).

percent for the nonpoor). Most of the property income of the poor is the imputed value of rent from their owner-occupied homes (see Chapter 9). Many of the nonpoor also own financial or other assets that earn cash income.

- Third, the poor receive a larger share of their income from transfers (21 percent) than the nonpoor. Nevertheless, although transfers account for only 16 percent of the income of the nonpoor, the nonpoor receive higher absolute amounts from pensions, and private transfers. The poor and nonpoor receive similar amounts in food rations and public transfers from the social protection net (see Chapter 9).

Because labor earnings comprise the largest component of household income, greater or lesser earnings are generally a key determinant of poverty. Analysis of poverty therefore begins with the labor market (Table 5.2 and Box 5.1).

Box 5.1. The Terminology of Labor Market Analysis

Terminology used in labor market analysis needs to be precise. As used here, *employment* refers to all income-generating activity based on labor, thus *working people* and *employed people* mean the same thing. This includes wage and nonwage activities. *Nonwage work* includes household-based agricultural work and other forms of self-employment, such as ownership of microenterprises. Following ILO usage, the term *labor force* refers to individuals who are either (*a*) working or (*b*) unemployed (not working, available to work and actively seeking work). In other words, all people in the total population are classified as either *in* the labor force (working, or unemployed) or *out* of the labor force. The *unemployment rate* is the share of the labor force that is unemployed (the unemployed population divided by the share participating in the labor force). When referring to the employment rate, total population is used as denominator. However, when referring to the unemployment rate, the denominator is those participating in the labor force. *Participation in the labor force* refers to people who are working or in the labor force but unemployed. A person is outside the labor force if they are not working, not available to work, and not actively seeking work. *Economic dependency ratio* is defined as the share of the population not working divided by the share of the population that is working. *Age dependency ratio* is defined as the share of the population under 15 years old divided by the share of the population over 15. The terms *labor income*, *labor earnings*, and *employment income* are used synonymously here.

Employment

About 38 percent of adult Iraqis are working. The remainder of adults are not working, either because they are unemployed (5 percent)[26] or not in the labor force (57 percent). Compared to the 67 percent average for lower-middle-income (LMI) countries, or to the rates of the other MENA countries shown in Figure 5.1, 38 percent is an exceptionally low share of working population. Indeed, the share of working adults ranks second from the bottom.

Figure 5.1. Share of Adults (15+ Years) Who Are Working, MENA (Percent)

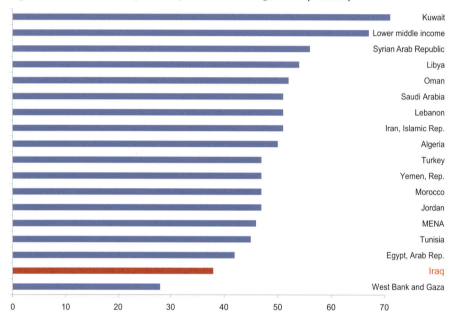

Sources: IHSES for Iraq, *World Development Indicators* (2008: CD version) for other countries

Labor force participation by poverty status, geographic area, and gender, Annex 5.1	Employment by poverty status, gender, geographic area, work sector, and place of employment , Annex 5.2	Unemployment by poverty status, gender, geographic area, work sector, and place of employment, Annex 5.3

[26] Five percent of all adults (aged 15 or over) are unemployed. The unemployment *rate*, however, is higher (12 percent). The unemployment rate is defined as the unemployed as a share of the labor force—that is, 5/(38 +5).

The low rate at which adults are working is particularly problematic because it is combined with the fact that Iraq has an unusually high proportion of its population who are children—that is, too young to work. Forty percent of Iraqis are under 15 years of age, compared to the 25 percent average for LMI countries—rates that are driven by Iraq's unusually high fertility of 4.3 births per woman compared to the LMI average of 2.1 births per woman. The combined effect of low adult employment and high fertility is that (on average) the labor income of each Iraqi worker supports four people. In contrast, in LMI countries as a whole, each worker supports less than a third as many.

This chapter focuses on adult employment issues; however, it is important to note at the outset that adult employment and fertility are related. Especially in urban areas, women face a trade-off between time spent working and time spent having and caring for children. These linkages, which are addressed in this chapter and in Chapter 7 on health and fertility, are intimately related to poverty.[27]

Female labor force participation

Why is the level of employment so low overall? The primary reason is Iraq's unusually low level of female employment. As shown in Table 5.3, only about 11 percent of adult women are employed, compared to about two-thirds of adult men.

This very large discrepancy is not explained by *un*employment, but by the fact that fully 87 percent of Iraqi women are not engaged in the labor force in the first place.

Table 5.3. Male and Female Employment (Percent in the Labor Force)

Employment	Men	Women	
In labor force			
Employed	66	11	
Unemployed	9	2	Female participation in the labor force, Annex 5.4
Subtotal	75	13	
Not in labor force	25	87	
Total	100	100	

Source: IHSES.

[27] Chapter 7 discusses fertility in the context of health. Annex 7.5 to that chapter includes statistical detail on basic household demography, as well as the share of the under-15 population by governorate and poverty status. In addition, Annex 7.6 provides an analytic note on the relationship between fertility ratios, fertility, and poverty status.

Figure 5.2 illustrates the male-female employment gap in comparative perspective. As shown, Iraq's 75 percent rate of *male* labor force participation is slightly below the 77 percent MENA average. That is low, though still within the normal range for the region overall. What is different in comparative terms is Iraq's 13 percent rate of *female* labor force participation, which is exceptionally low compared with that of its neighbors.

Figure 5.2. Male and Female Labor Force Participation in Iraq and Comparator Countries (Percent)

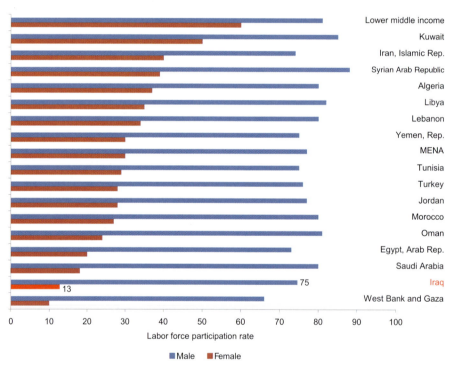

Source: World Development Indicators (2008: CD version), and IHSES.

If women are disproportionately outside the labor force in Iraq, what are they doing instead? For the most part, they are spending time caring for their (generally large) families. Iraqi women tend to marry early (about 9 percent of women marry by age 15 and 27 percent by18 according to the Iraq Family Health Survey).They tend to remain married and have large families. By the end of their childbearing years, Iraqi women on average have experienced 6.4 live births (IFHS), with much higher rates among rural and less-educated women.

To understand the trade-offs among work and nonwork activities, IHSES included a module on time use for individuals older than 10 years. As might be expected, women's time is largely accounted for by in-home activities. On average women spend 242 minutes per day doing housework, food preparation, and childcare (compared to less than 10 minutes per day for men). By contrast, men spend 234 minutes per day working and commuting to work (compared to 28 minutes per day for women).

Men's activities / women's activities— Time use on work and nonwork activities, Annex 5.4.1

Multivariate regression was used to analyze the factors that predict women's participation in the labor force. While education emerged as the strongest predictor overall, its effects are weaker than might have been expected and far from uniform across the female population. Why?

Box 5.2. Alternative Explanations for Low Employment

Aside from low female participation in the labor force, what other factors might explain Iraq's unusually low level of overall employment? Two alternative explanations were considered—first, the rate of *un*employment, and second, the security situation.

Unusually high **un***employment*. A low rate of employment could be explained by a high rate of unemployment—in other words, many people not working but looking for work. While Iraq's 12 percent unemployment rate is higher than desirable, it is still below MENA's average overall unemployment rate of 14 percent. Given that Iraq's overall rate of labor force participation is also below the MENA average, *un*employment does not therefore explain low employment. (See Annex 5.3.1 on unemployment.)

The security situation. Could Iraqis be staying away from or not be looking for work because of the security situation? This seems like a plausible explanation since IHSES fieldwork was launched at the peak of civilian violence in October-November 2006. However, evidence to support this hypothesis is weak. First, direct questionnaire responses were examined. Second, governorate-level employment data were combined with security data from the Iraq Body Count Web site and with IHSES respondents' reported experiences with violence. Effects emerged but were small and not robust. Interestingly, female employment (as well as female school attendance) appeared to have been relatively less affected by the security situation than men's. (See Annex 5.3.2 on security as explanation for low employment.)

Figure 5.3 shows years of education and predicted probability of labor force participation for rural and urban women. Three points stand out. First, the impact of education on urban women is very strong; however, it kicks in only at the university level. Within urban areas very few women with less than a university education participate in the labor force, in contrast to very high rates of participation among women with university educations. Second, education has a much smaller impact on labor force participation among rural women. Third, rural women with less than post-secondary education are more likely to participate in the labor force than their urban counterparts.

Figure 5.3. Years of Education and Probability of Labor Force Participation among Rural and Urban Women

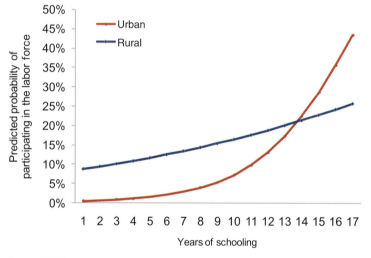

Source· IHSES.

Labor force participation is closely related to the low financial returns to education. Additional years of schooling have negligible effect on wages until university level (see Chapter 6). Thus, the IHSES questionnaire response—"family not interested"—reflects many parents' common (but unfortunately accurate) assessment of the financial benefits that accrue to additional years of schooling.[28]

---

[28] Although financial benefits of education are small in Iraq, nonfinancial benefits may be large. Analysis from other countries shows that large nonfinancial returns accrue to girls' education, including lower fertility and improved health and education of the children they later bear.

Productivity and Types of Work Performed

Although Iraqi employment rates are low by international standards, low rates of employment do not explain why some Iraqis are poor and others are not. First, poor and nonpoor adults are both employed at approximately the same rate (about 38 percent); and second, the poor and nonpoor work nearly an identical number of hours per week and an identical number of months per year.[29]

The difference is not employment per se but the productivity of employment. As measured by earnings per hour, nonpoor workers earn fully a third more than poor workers (Figure 5.4). The difference in total remuneration is considerably

Figure 5.4. Work Performed by Poor and Nonpoor Workers (Percent)

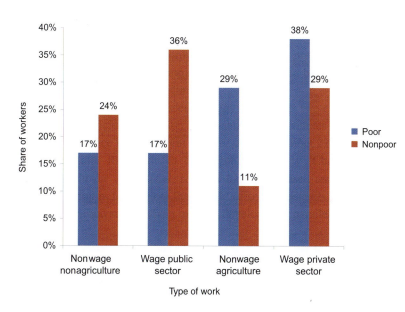

Source: IHSES.

---

[29] The poor work an average of 37.8 hours per week, compared to 38.4 for the nonpoor. The poor work an average of 11.3 months per year, exactly the same as the 11.3 average for the nonpoor. Few Iraqi workers (about 7 percent) hold more than one job, which includes the poor (8.2 percent) as well as the nonpoor (6.8 percent).

larger due to the fact that poor workers are much less likely to receive job-related benefits such as pensions and medical insurance.[30]

Figure 5.4 shows that the poor tend to work in lower productivity sectors. And, as demonstrated in the section on agriculture below, the poor have lower productivity (earnings per hour worked) than the nonpoor even within the same type of work.[31]

Four points about poor workers stand out.

- Nearly a third are engaged in nonwage agriculture. This category (discussed in more detail in the following section) refers to those who work on family-owned land and whose labor income comes from the sale of farm products (rather than wages).[32] In rural areas, 52 percent of poor workers belong to this category. By contrast, only 11 percent of nonpoor workers are employed in nonwage agriculture.
- Thirty-eight percent of the poor work for wages in the private sector—nearly half in construction, a particularly active sector in light of ongoing reconstruction efforts.
- Among poor Iraqis, relatively few work in nonwage nonagriculture, a category that refers to all self-employment activities outside of agriculture. By contrast, nearly a quarter of the nonpoor perform such entrepreneurial work.[33]
- Relatively few poor Iraqis work in the public sector (including state-owned enterprises). This is perhaps surprising in a country with a public sector as large as Iraq's. However, public sector jobs are largely held by the top decile; nearly half of workers in the top decile are in the public sector.

---

[30] Only 15 percent of poor workers receive job benefits compared to 34 percent of nonpoor workers. Among poor workers 58 percent work for wages, of whom only 26 percent receive benefits. Of all Iraqi workers, 68 percent work for wages, 50 percent of whom receive benefits. For the average Iraqi worker, 66 percent are in wage jobs, of which 46 percent are covered by job benefits. In other words, 30 percent of all Iraqi workers are covered by job benefits. (See details in Annex 5.2 and Annex 9.2.)

[31] Those relatively few women who participate in the labor force are heavily concentrated in public sector wage jobs (especially urban, nonpoor, educated women) and in nonwage agriculture (especially rural, poor, less educated women). Among poor working women, 78 percent are in nonwage agriculture, 11 percent in public wage jobs, 8 percent in nonwage nonagricultural jobs, and only 3 percent in private sector wage jobs. Among nonpoor working women, 22 percent are in nonwage agriculture, 66 percent are in public sector wage jobs, 9 percent are in nonwage, nonagriculture jobs, and 3 percent are in private-sector wage jobs.

[32] Only 10 percent of those working in agriculture are wage workers.

[33] About half of all entrepreneurs are in the wholesale or retail trade. Of enterprises owned by the poor, only 7 percent have employees, compared to 21 percent among the nonpoor.

Agriculture

Relative to its roughly 5 percent share of GDP, agriculture is particularly important as an element in poverty reduction. Agriculture represents a disproportionate share of total employment among the poor, and an even larger share among the poorest of the poor.

Agriculture—
Basic indicators
and rural livelihood,
Annex 5.7

Among workers in nonwage agriculture, the average income per hour among poor workers is less than half that of nonpoor workers despite the fact that both groups tend to work on their own land. Poor and nonpoor farmers are generally similar in their forms of land tenure and in the kinds of crops and livestock they raise. There is no single explanation for their differences in productivity; however, these appear primarily related to education, market access, and the generally dow quality of poor farmers' land.[34]

Both poor and nonpoor farmers have suffered from the productivity decline of recent decades. The United Nations and the World Bank estimated average declines in output of about 1.1 percent annually between 1988 and 2003. These declines occurred in virtually every area of traditional agricultural production. For example, the Joint Iraq Needs Assessment (October 2003) reports that the yield of wheat, a staple crop since antiquity, has dropped to about 680 kilograms per hectare—a level that is now less than a quarter of some neighboring countries. Similarly, rice production plummeted from about 2.2 tons per hectare in 1991 to 0.9 tons per hectare in 2002.

Economic activities—
How and where the
poor earn income,
Annex 5.6

---

[34] Poor workers in nonwage agriculture have far higher illiteracy rates (34 percent) than the average poor worker (22 percent) or the average nonpoor worker (11 percent). Poor workers in nonwage agriculture are more likely than nonpoor workers to live on unpaved roads (86 percent versus 75 percent), or to live more than five kilometers from a market (61 percent versus 45 percent). And, while poor nonwage agricultural workers are actually more likely to own their own land (79 percent compared to 73 percent), these poor nonwage workers own less land (5.3 hectares versus 6.9 hectares), and they cultivate a smaller share of the land (72 percent versus 76 percent). The smaller share of land cultivated by the poor is likely an indication of owning lower-quality land. (Note that 5.3 hectares is equivalent to 21.2 donums and that 6.9 hectares is equivalent to 27.5 donums.)

The decline in agricultural productivity has multiple causes—decades of underinvestment and neglect, distortions in domestic demand and agricultural pricing from food subsidies and imports, and the impact of environmental degradation. Publicly owned irrigation infrastructure, for example, was all but abandoned after imposition of sanctions in the early 1990s. By the early 2000s, institutions undertaking agricultural research, extension services, animal health, production support, plant quarantines, and disease control had already deteriorated, then suffered even greater damage during the invasion of 2003 and its aftermath.

The deterioration of Iraq's water resources has been particularly severe in recent years. Droughts during 2007, 2008, and 2009 have been the worst in recent memory. Water flow from Iraq's once-great rivers has slowed to a trickle in some places, a complex phenomenon with many causes—increased demand for water in rapidly growing cities, inefficient and outdated irrigation infrastructure, natural drought conditions, and upstream restrictions on water flow from Syria and Turkey. Many of the poorest rural areas of Iraq (in Kerbela and Basrah, for example; see Chapter 4) are precisely those where the water shortages have been most severe.

Most of Iraq's agricultural land is now classified as degraded or seriously degraded. Reasons include poor drainage, overgrazing, and perverse incentives that encouraged nonsustainable cereal cultivation. Subsidies for fertilizers have greatly encouraged their overapplication, with consequent losses to longer-term productivity. Other forms of environmental contamination have been widespread. These have had deleterious impact not only on agricultural productivity, but on a host of rural health problems, such as the increased cancer rates observed in Basrah.

An Economy That Produces Jobs, Not Just Oil

The preceding discussion makes clear that employment and income (and hence the likelihood of poverty) are mirrors of what the economy offers its workers. In Iraq, most employment opportunities, such as they are, are in stagnant low-productivity sectors where additional education creates little comparative advantage.

Sources of income, by poverty status and geographic area, Annex 5.5

It should be noted that the scarcity of well-paying high-productivity jobs is by no means unique to those below the poverty line. It also explains the relative absence of wealth *above* the poverty line; and taken together, the absence of opportunity at both ends of the spectrum is the main explanation for Iraq's remarkably low level of Gini inequality. As discussed in Chapter 3, misinvestment of resources over the past 25 years led to a one-third drop in average in GDP per capita, a trend that stands in marked contrast to positive growth for every other country in the region. Although Iraq's inequality is among the lowest in the world, inequality in this case is not attributable to long-term investments in human capital or productive infrastructure, but to policies that reshaped the economy by flattening opportunity and depressing growth.

From this perspective, oil has been a mixed blessing. As illustrated in Figure 5.5, oil represents more than half of GDP but less than 1 percent of all employment. Taken together, agriculture, manufacturing, and services represents less than half of GDP, but nearly all jobs—and by extension, the welfare of the very large population that is directly dependent on those jobs. The figure points to the fundamental challenge that Iraq faces: economic and policy reforms to generate higher-productivity jobs, coupled with investments in education and health to help citizens raise employment capacities.

Figure 5.5. Share of Employment and Share of GDP, by Sector (Percent)

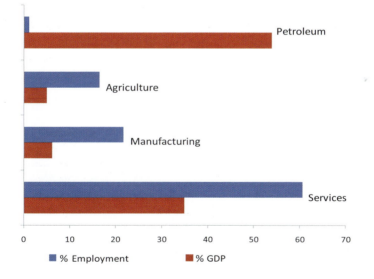

Sources: IHSES for employment; COSIT national accounts data for GDP structure

47

Role of the Private Sector

The private sector, which accounts for all but 17 percent of the jobs of the poor, faces many obstacles. Overall, Iraq ranks 153rd out of 183 countries on the World Bank's 2010 ease-of-doing-business ranking. Starting businesses and obtaining credit are particularly problematic since startups are typically financed through savings and personal loans (see Annex 9.3). Domestic credit is only 2.6 percent of GDP. The legal and regulatory systems are slow and unclear, and enforcement is unpredictable. While the National Investment Law of 2006 provides a good basis for a modern legal structure defining the rights of investors and providing tax incentives, it has yet to be fully implemented. Private enterprises, like individual homeowners, suffer from the erratic provision of electricity, interruptions in water supply, a deficient road system, and frequent breakdowns in telecommunication services (see Chapter 8).

Chapter 6

Education

Deterioration in Education

Over the past generation, educational attainment in Iraq has fallen precipitously. Primary school enrollment fell from 99 percent in 1980 to 77 percent in 2006. Similarly, net secondary enrollments dropped from 91 percent in 1985 to 89 percent in 1990 and 86 percent in 2000.[35] As shown in Table 6.1, young men are actually less likely to be literate than their fathers. Whereas Iraqi enrollment rates were the highest in the region a generation ago, today they are among the lowest (Figures 6.1 and 6.2).

Figure 6.1. Net Primary School Enrollment in MENA, 2006 (Percent)

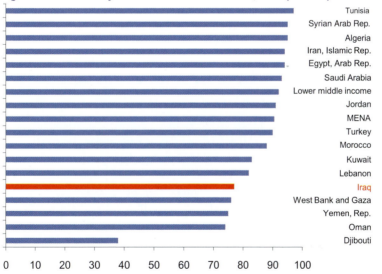

Source: World Development Indicators (2008: CD version). Data are from 2006 or most recent year available.

Literacy and enrollment by poverty status, gender, and geographic area, Annex 6.1	Iraq and comparators— Educational indicators in comparative perspective, Annex 6.2	Physical access, distance to schools, Annex 6.3

---

[35] See UNESCO for 1985 and 1990 data, and *WDI* (2008) for 2000 data.

Table 6.1. Key Educational Indicators

Literacy

	15–24 years (%)	35–44 years (%)
Males	88	93
Female	81	75
Both	85	84

	Nonpoor (%)			Poor (%)		
	Urban	Rural	All	Urban	Rural	All
Primary, males	91	86	90	80	79	80
Primary, females	90	78	87	82	60	70
Intermediate, males	50	33	46	25	23	24
Intermediate, females	45	21	39	25	11	17
Secondary-age males	29	18	26	12	9	11
Secondary-age females	26	10	23	20	4	12

Net enrollment rates

	Iraq	MENA	LMI
Primary	77	82	93
Secondary	38	67	67

Kilometers to nearest school

	Percent < 1 km.	Percent < 5 km.
Primary school	89	99
Middle or secondary	70	90

Student-teacher ratio in primary schools

Iraq	MENA	LMI
17 to 1	23 to 1	19 to 1

Female-to-male ratio in primary schools

Iraq	MENA	LMI
.78	.94	.98

Returns to education (%)

Each additional year of schooling raises
average hourly wages by: 2.6 percent (Iraq), versus 6.0 percent (international average).

Government spending on education (%)

	Iraq	MENA
Education as share of total government budget	6	18
Investment as a % of education budget	2	6
Nonsalary as % of recurrent education budget	11	19

Average out-of-pocket expenditure per household

	Average monthly spending (ID 000)	Monthly expenditure as a share of PCE at the poverty line (%)
Primary student	8,000	10
Intermediate students	14,300	19
Secondary students	25,500	33

Sources: IHSES, World Bank, and *World Development Indicators* (2008: CD version).

Note: To allow comparisons among varying educational systems, *WDI* categorizes education as primary, secondary, and tertiary. Iraqi intermediate school is classified as secondary whenever compared with other countries.

Within Iraq, an internationally familiar pattern prevails: the poor have lower enrollment rates than the nonpoor; girls have lower enrollment rates than boys; and residents of rural areas have lower enrollment rates than residents of urban areas (Figure 6.3). These gaps are small at the primary level but become larger at higher levels.[36] By the intermediate level, the enrollment rate for poor girls in rural areas is only 11 percent.

Figure 6.2. Net Secondary School Enrollment in MENA, 2006 (Percent)

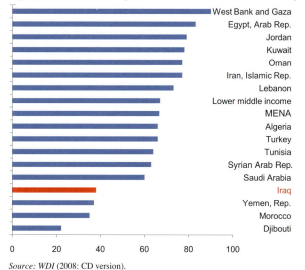

Source: WDI (2008: CD version).

Figure 6.3. Intermediate School Enrollment Rates, by Gender and Urban/Rural Location (Percent)

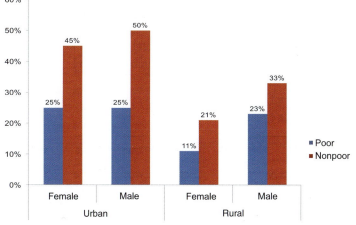

[36] The Iraqi educational system includes primary school for ages 6–11, intermediate school for ages 12–14, and secondary school for ages 15–17. Iraqi intermediate school is classified as secondary school where comparisons are made with UNESCO or *World Development Indicators* data.

Perhaps contrary to expectations, low enrollment rates are *not* principally due to lack of access to facilities or lack of teachers. Nearly 90 percent of Iraqi children live within a kilometer of a primary school, and 99 percent within five kilometers. About 70 percent live within a kilometer of an intermediate or secondary school, and 90 percent within five kilometers. Of those with unenrolled children, only 11 percent cited travel difficulty as a reason. Moreover, Iraq has very low student-teacher ratios—approximately 17 primary school students for every primary school teacher (compared to the lower-middle-income country average of 19 to 1 and the MENA country average of 23 to 1).[37] Nor were low enrollment rates for the population overall explained by the security situation: while lack of security decreases the probability of enrollment at primary and intermediate levels, the larger pattern of declining enrollment rates had clearly been underway for at least two decades before IHSES went to the field in 2006–07.

Insufficient Public Spending, Low Quality

Enrollment rates and their determinants, Annex 6.4

The principal cause of low enrollment is not hard to understand: deteriorating quality (and value) of the education that is offered. The proximate cause is neglect.

Public investment in education has been low for several decades. From an average of US$623 per student in 1989, expenditure plunged to just US$35 per student by 2003. As a result, school infrastructure massively deteriorated as maintenance and new construction were deferred year after year. Teacher training, curricular modernization, monitoring and assessment, and introduction of new teaching techniques were increasingly rare. More recently, facilities were damaged and trained teachers fled the country during the 2003 invasion and the subsequent violence.

Iraqi authorities have begun to increase the education budget. By 2006, expenditure had risen to US$253 per student. This still represents only about a third the expenditure level of the late 1980s in absolute terms, and in real terms significantly less.

---

[37] The low national-level student-teacher ratio hides substantial variations at the governorate level and within the six districts of Baghdad. In 2006, Ninevah Governorate had a ratio (about 29 students per teacher) that was almost three times the ratios in Wasit and Missan governorates (about 12 students per teacher). Within Baghdad Governorate, the highest ratio is in Rasafa (25 students per teacher) and the lowest in Kark (16 students per teacher). See "Public Expenditure and Institutional Assessment: Public Financial Management in a Conflict-Affected Environment." World Bank, Washington, DC, 2008.

Despite the increased spending, the ratio of the education budget to the overall public budget (6 percent) is still only about a third of the regional average (18 percent).

Public spending on education, Annex 6.5

Current spending is not well balanced with respect to teacher salaries, materials, and training, and to capital investment. Salaries in 2007 accounted for more than 90 percent of operational expenditure. The wage bill has risen substantially from both salary increases and the massive recruitment of new staff, which largely explains the relatively low student-teacher ratios. This does not, however, necessarily imply more and better teachers in the classroom, or adequate replacement of the very large number of teachers who fled or were displaced.

The low share of nonsalary recurrent expenditure by the Ministry of Education (5 percent of the educational operating budget) represents little more than half the average of other MENA countries. Investment in aspects of education other than salaries is extremely low as a share of spending. Spending on salaries at this level crowds out resources for inputs such as curricular materials and in-service teacher training needed to improve quality. Compounding matters, in 2006 only 14 percent of the nonsalary recurrent budget in education was spent and fully 88 percent of that amount went to security-related equipment and services.

Only 2 percent of the education budget was allocated to capital investment in 2006—quite low compared with other MENA countries, which on average allocate approximately 6 percent to capital improvements. There was a large jump in the capital investment budget in 2007. However, only a small portion of this was spent. Reflecting this ongoing underinvestment in education, about a third of Iraqi schools run double or even triple shifts. Facilities remain in poor condition, often lacking basic services such as electricity.

The low quality of the educational offering is evidenced by unusually low returns to education (that is, increased earnings attributed to additional years of schooling). Holding other factors constant, a wage earner's average hourly earnings increases *at most*[38] 2.6 percent for each

Estimating returns to education, main models and robustness of tests, Annex 6.6

additional year of schooling. (Internationally, returns to education average around 6 percent.[39])

---

[38] The term *at most* is used here because, if anything, the estimated 2.6 percent increase in salary attributed to one additional year of education *over*states the return to education in Iraq since the methodology controls for experience, gender, sector of work, and location, but not for ability. Years of schooling are used as a proxy for ability. More direct measures for ability would almost certainly reduce the estimated coefficient for returns to education.

The hourly wage returns from schooling are shown in Figure 6.4. Wage rates for persons who have completed secondary education are virtually identical to those who are illiterate. Even a university education provides surprisingly little wage advantage. Hourly earnings do not begin to rise substantially until postgraduate education, a level realistically obtainable for only a tiny minority of the workforce.

Not only are returns low, but sending a child to school entails real costs despite the nominally free tuition. Out-of-pocket spending per student averages an amount equivalent to about 10 percent of PCE at the poverty line for primary school students. This rises to about a third of the poverty line for secondary students. (Uniforms account for about half the cost, with books another 20–25 percent.) At the secondary level, transportation costs are relatively higher due to generally greater average distances from home to school. Regression analysis of the determinants of enrollment showed that being poor significantly reduces a child's probability of being enrolled by 5 percentage points at the primary level and nearly 12 percentage points at the intermediate level.[40]

Figure 6.4. Median Hourly Wage, by Education Level (ID 000)

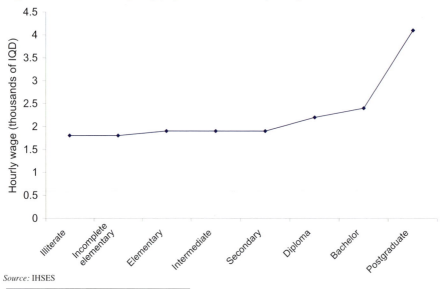

Source: IHSES

[39] See C. Harmon, H. Oosterbeek, and I. Walker, "The Returns to Education: A Review of the Evidence, Issues, and Deficiencies in the Literature," Centre for the Economics of Education, London School of Economics, London, 2000.

[40] The coefficient on poverty likely reflects the importance of both out-of-pocket expenses and the opportunity cost of children's time. Nationwide child labor rates are relatively low (less than 2 percent of those aged 6–11 years and less than 8 percent of those aged 12–14 years). However, about 18 percent of rural 12–14-year-old boys work (vs. 9 percent of urban boys). Few girls of this age work, though 48 percent of 12–14-year-old girls in rural areas and 33 percent of those in urban areas perform household chores more than three hours per day.

Chapter 7

Health and Fertility

Deterioration in Health

Although Iraqi health indicators were once among the best in the region, the health status of the population has deteriorated over the past three decades and is now low overall. The impact of recent changes is sadly captured in Table 7.1, which shows changing life expectancy for the MENA region since 1980. For countries such as Egypt, Oman, the Republic of Yemen, and Libya, average life expectancy climbed by nearly 15 years. Only in Iraq did life expectancy decline, falling by about 3 years.

The decline in life expectancy reflects a parallel reversal in the broader health status of the population (Table 7.2). While war and civilian violence have had tragic health consequences, low Iraqi health status has deeper roots and now affects the entire population, particularly children, in every region of the country.

Infant mortality is now above both the MENA and LMI averages. Roughly 15 percent of babies are born at low birth weight (less than 2.5 kilograms), greatly increasing their risk of death in the first months of life. Nearly 40 percent of Iraqi newborns are not protected against neonatal tetanus. Moreover, within Iraq infant mortality and low birth weight are both associated with poverty status (see Annex 7.1 for data at the governorate level).

The situation for children under age five is more mixed. Iraq does reasonably well for immunization coverage and the use

Table 7.1. Changing Life Expectancy in MENA, 1980–2006

Country	Life expectancy in years		Change (no. years) between 1980–2006
	1980	2006	
Egypt, Arab Rep.	55	71	+16
Oman	61	76	+15
Yemen, Rep.	47	62	+15
Libya	60	74	+14
Morocco	58	71	+13
Tunisia	62	74	+12
Saudi Arabia	61	73	+12
Algeria	60	72	+12
Iran, Islamic Rep.	59	71	+12
Syrian Arab Rep.	63	74	+11
Turkey	61	71	+10
Jordan	63	72	+9
Kuwait	71	78	+7
Djibouti	48	54	+6
Lebanon	67	72	+5
Iraq	**61**	**58**	**−3**

Source: *WDI* (2008: CD version).

Table 7.2 Key Health and Fertility Indicators

Life expectancy and fertility indicators

	Iraq	MENA	LMI
Life expectancy [a]	58 years	70 years	71 years
Fertility [b]	4.3	2.0	2.1

Exposure to traumatic event during lifetime: 56% (e.g., police/army search, exposure to shooting or bomb blast, internal displacement, witnessing a killing) [c]

Neonatal health

Infant mortality (deaths by first birthday)
Iraq: 35 deaths per 1,000 live births
MENA average: 34 per 1,000 live births
LMI average: 27 per 1,000 live births

Low birth weight [d]
Iraq: 15%
MENA average: 12%
LMI average: 7%

Infants protected from neonatal tetanus [e]
Iraq: 61%

Child health and nutrition

Under-five mortality
Iraq: 41 per 1,000
MENA average: 42 per 1,000
LMI average: 36 per 1,000

Stunted growth among children under 5
Among poor children: 26%
Among nonpoor children: 20%
MENA average: 26%
LMI average: 25%

Underweight among children under 5
Among poor children: 10%
Among nonpoor children: 7%
MENA average: 17 %
LMI average: 11%

Wasting among children under 5
Among poor children: 5.5%
Among nonpoor children: 4.4%
MENA average: 8%

Access (in distance)

Within 10 kms. of medical center or doctor			*Within 10 kms. of public hospital*		
	Rural	Urban		Rural	Urban
Nonpoor	82%	99%	Nonpoor	45%	92%
Poor	76%	99%	Poor	40%	88%

Utilization

Share receiving medical attention for a reported illness or injury
Poor: 95%   Nonpoor: 95%
Share receiving medical attention for a reported chronic disease
Poor: 77%   Nonpoor: 84%

Government spending on health

Government health spending as share of total government expenditure
Iraq: 3.4%   MENA average: 8.2%   LMI average: 5.9%

Out-of-pocket spending by households

Avg. expenditure per month for an illness or injury: ID 23,800
Poor: ID 17,800   Nonpoor: ID 24,800

Notes: MENA refers to the Middle East and North Africa; LMI refers to lower-middle-income countries.

a. Life expectancy at birth indicates the number of years a newborn infant would live if prevailing patterns of mortality at the time of birth were to stay the same throughout his or her life.

b. Total fertility rate represents the number of children that would be born to a woman if she were to live to the end of her childbearing years and bear children in accordance with current age-specific fertility rates.

c. Lifetime exposure to trauma is taken from the Iraq Mental Health Survey Report (Government of Iraq [GOI] and WHO). The methodology and definitions are from the World Mental Health Survey Initiative.

d. Low birth weight (less than 2,500 grams) indicates an increased risk of dying during an infant's early months and years. Those who survive face increased risks throughout their lives.

e. Pregnant women are given the tetanus toxoid vaccine to prevent maternal tetanus and neonatal tetanus, both of which are major causes of mortality. Iraq's current rate of 61% coverage can be compared to Algeria, 70%; the Arab Republic of Egypt, 86%; Kuwait, 90%; Lebanon, 72%; Oman, 94%; the Syrian Arab Republic, 87%; Tunisia, 89%; Turkey, 67%, and Saudi Arabia, 56% (*World Development Indicators*, 2009: CD version) or Algeria, 70%, Djibouti, 77%, the Islamic Republic of Iran, 83%, Jordan, 87%; Morocco, 85%; Oman, 95%; the Syrian Arab Republic, 92%; Tunisia, 96%; and the Republic of Yemen, 52% (WHO data, 2007).

Maternal, newborn, and child health indicators, Annex 7.1	Adult health indicators, Annex 7.2	Access and utilization, Annex 7.3
Spending on health, Annex 7.4	Fertility and reproductive health, Annex 7.5	Dependency ratios, fertility, and poverty status, Annex 7.6

of oral rehydration solution to treat diarrheal disease, as do most other countries in the region. For example, the immunization rates for tuberculosis, polio, and DPT in Iraq exceed 93 percent of all children under age 5 (IHSES, Tabulation Report: Table 4-16).

Data on child malnutrition have been inconsistent over the years. Yet disagreements over specific numbers aside, virtually all experts agree, first, that malnutrition levels rose significantly during the 1990s; and second, that malnutrition continues to be a serious problem (although child malnutrition is now below the MENA average). Within Iraq, malnutrition is higher among the poor than the nonpoor. Of course the presence of *any* childhood malnutrition may seem surprising in light of near 100 percent coverage of the public food distribution system, which alone supplies on average 85 percent of required calories.

Reminiscent of the story in education, health status is low despite public health services that are widely accessible and ostensibly free. Whether poor or nonpoor, virtually all urban households live within 10 kilometers of a free (or nearly free) government health center. Even among rural households, 80 percent live within 10 kilometers of a health service center, and 21 percent within 10 kilometers of a public hospital.

In addition to having good physical access, Iraqis also tend to *use* health services. Among the poor and nonpoor alike, 95 percent reported receiving medical attention for the illnesses or injuries.

Insufficient Public Spending, Low Quality

This raises a crucial question: If medical services are physically available, if government health services are ostensibly free, if the population is accustomed to utilizing health services, and if food rations are universally distributed, why then have health indicators gone down so dramatically?

The answer in the area of health is roughly the same as in education (Chapter 6): low quality of services offered related to a several-decade legacy of neglect. Year after year, infrastructure deficits accumulated as necessary investments were deferred. In addition, Iraq's human resources in medicine and health have been badly depleted. Currently, there are 2 health professionals per 1,000 population—about 1.2 nurses, 0.6 physicians, and 0.2 midwives and other trained personnel. This compares with an average of 1.0 nurses and 1.3 physicians per 1,000 population in lower-middle-income countries. By way of comparison, the World Health Organization (WHO) recommends at least 2.5 healthcare professionals per 1,000 population as a minimum standard for adequate care. For lower-middle-income countries, the overall average is 2.3 per 1,000.

Physicians and other skilled health workers first began to leave Iraq during the 1990s as salaries started to decline. That loss accelerated as the security situation deteriorated. Indeed, one Ministry of Health study estimates that as many as half the national medical staff fled the country in recent years. Moreover, those who were trained subsequently received less-adequate as a result of Iraq's prolonged international isolation. Within steady deterioration in both the physical and human infrastructure, it is not surprising that quality of medical care and health outcomes have worsened.

Consider the consequences in just one area—prenatal care. The Iraq Family Health Survey (2006/07) found that 84 percent of pregnant women sought prenatal care. Yet of these, only 60 percent were weighed; only 63 percent had urine samples taken; only 66 percent had blood samples taken; and only 76 percent had their blood pressure measured—a standard of care far below well-established international norms. Not surprisingly, only 56 percent of pregnant women who sought prenatal care returned for the four visits that are considered minimally necessary for adequate prenatal care (MICS).

Evidence indicates that the poor receive even lower-quality care than the nonpoor. Among poor women who received antenatal care, 54 percent were not weighed (compared to 40 percent among the nonpoor); 48 percent did not have a urine specimen taken (compared to 37 percent among the nonpoor); and 46 percent did not have a blood sample taken (compared to 33 percent among the nonpoor).

Unlike the case of education, however, there is an alternative to public health services in Iraq. The population has access to private services, though at a higher cost. When they are ill or injured, most Iraqis *do* seek medical care (Table 7.1). However, neither the poor nor the nonpoor favor general practitioners or primary services. Both groups report high use of specialist physicians, who they generally see at private clinics. Even among the poor, more than 35 percent consulted specialist doctors and private hospitals, while fewer than 20 percent used public medical centers.

Private specialist care comes at a high cost. The average out-of-pocket expenditure per month for those experiencing an illness or injury is ID 23,800 (ID 17,800 for the poor and ID 24,800 for the nonpoor). The largest part of this outlay is for medicines (36 percent), followed by hospital fees and consultations (26 percent), and accessibility to medical services (14 percent). Treating an illness therefore represents a major household expenditure—equivalent to between a quarter and a third of PCE expenditure at the poverty line. For a household that is already close to the poverty line—that is to say, most Iraqi households—episodes of illness, even relatively minor illnesses, are paid for at the risk of poverty.

In recent years, public spending on health has risen. Nevertheless, it remains low by regional standards. As a share of total government expenditure, public health accounts for 3.4 percent of the Iraqi budget. This compares with the MENA average of 8.2 percent and the LMI average of 5.9 percent.

Fertility, Dependency Ratios, and Poverty

Under the previous regime, especially in the 1980s, population growth was encouraged. This included prohibition of contraceptives, giving priority to married people in housing and employment, and offering material incentives for more children. Low contraception rates are an enduring legacy—about 50 percent of sexually active women compared to 76 percent in LMI and 60 percent in MENA countries (COSIT/UNICEF Multiple Indicators Cluster Survey of 2006). Iraq's fertility rate is correspondingly high (4.3)—more than twice the MENA (2.0) and LMI (2.1) averages (Figure 7.1). Fertility rates in Iraq closely resemble the fertility rates of some of the poorest countries in the world.

There is little unmet demand for contraception—only 12 percent in rural areas and 10 percent in urban areas. MICS 2006 queried women's reasons for not using contraception. "Wanting more children" was the most commonly cited response, followed by "health reasons."

Figure 7.1. Fertility Rates: MENA and Lower-Middle-Income Countries

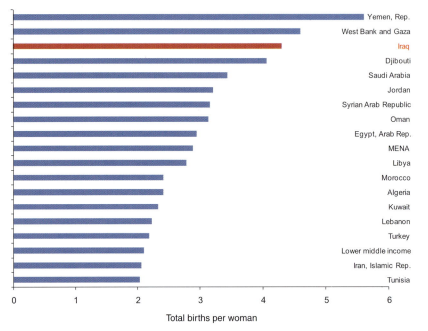

Total births per woman

Sources: Iraq data from UNICEF Multiple Indicator Cluster Surveys–Round 3; all other countries from *WDI*, 2008.

Figure 7.2 provides a stylized representation of the relationship between fertility and living standards. In this dynamic, high fertility translates into high economic dependency ratios (a large number of nonworking household members dependent on each working member) through multiple channels. First, high fertility has a direct impact on economic dependency by increasing the share of children in the population. Second, women who are not in the labor force have significantly more children than those who are employed (especially in urban areas where combining work and family responsibilities are most difficult). A high economic dependency ratio in turn affects the per capita expenditure that each household member can afford with any given income. Indirect effects, such as those acting through women's education, further reinforce the relationships between poverty and fertility.

As shown in Table 7.3, there are 3 children for every woman in the poorest decile, compared to 1.1 children for every woman in the richest. There are 1.6 children for every working-aged adult in the poorest decile, compared to 0.6 in the richest. As a result of this dynamic, there are 5 nonworking household members for every working person in the poorest decile—more than twice that of the richest

Figure 7.2.
Social Dynamics of Fertility and Living Standards

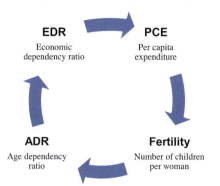

decile (2.3).[41] Thus, even if the wages of poor workers were as high as those of nonpoor workers, labor earnings per capita among the poor would be only half that of the nonpoor.

Table 7.3. Per Capita Expenditure (PCE) Deciles and Dependency Rates

PCE decile	Child-woman ratio in Iraq	Age dependency ratio	Economic dependency ratio
1	3.0	1.6	5.0
2	2.8	1.3	4.5
3	2.6	1.2	4.7
4	2.4	1.2	4.5
5	2.2	1.1	4.2
6	2.1	1.0	3.9
7	1.9	1.0	3.6
8	1.7	0.9	3.4
9	1.5	0.8	3.0
10	1.1	0.6	2.3

Source: IHSES

---

[41] The age dependency ratio shown here refers to household members under 15 or over 64 years of age, divided by household members 15–64 years old. The results are similar whether the elderly are included in the numerator or in the denominator. Note also that the number of children per woman is used here as a proxy for fertility. For more discussion, refer to Annex 7.6 in the supplementary volume to this report.

Chapter 8

Housing, Infrastructure, and Living Conditions

Housing

Quality of physical infrastructure is related to both the productivity of the economy and quality of life. Iraq made significant infrastructure investments in the 1980s and into the 1990s; however, with few exceptions, these were poorly maintained and have been further degraded by the subsequent instability. Although substantial reconstruction expenditures have been made since 2003, success has been mixed; and most services have not yet been restored to their pre-2003 levels, much less extended to underserved populations in disadvantaged geographic areas. (Table 8.1).

The IHSES Tabulation Report provides extensive data on the topics described in this chapter.

Home ownership and expenditure on housing

The vast majority of Iraqis own the homes they live in. Home ownership among the poor (82 percent) is higher than among the nonpoor (78 percent), because the poor are more likely to live in rural areas where homeownership is high relative to urban areas. Expenditure on housing accounts for 17 percent of total expenditure of

There are significant regional differences within Iraq in the quality of the built environment. Annex 8.1 through Annex 8.4 report on the following topics in detail:
- The cost of housing
- Overcrowding
- Home ownership
- Types of dwellings
- Electricity sources and reliability
- Domestic water sources and reliability
- Sanitation services
- Physical materials used for floors, walls, ceilings
- Paved roads

Table 8.1. Summary Housing and Infrastructure Indicators

Population who own their own homes (%)

Overall: 79

	Poor	*Nonpoor*
Urban	73	74
Rural	90	89

Share of expenditure spent on housing: Poor 17%, nonpoor 21%

Population living on dirt roads (%)

	Poor	*Nonpoor*
Urban	66	60
Rural	90	83

Population connected to public water supply (%)

Overall: 81

Poor: 67

Nonpoor: 86

Households reporting stable and sufficient water supply
Urban poor : 3 Urban nonpoor: 14
Rural poor: 6   Rural nonpoor: 12

Access to improved water source: Iraq, 81; MENA, 89; LMI, 71

Access to public sewerage or septic tanks (%)

Overall: 77

Urban poor: 79 Urban nonpoor: 86
Rural poor: 51 Rural nonpoor: 61

Access to improved sanitation: Iraq, 79; MENA, 76; LMI, 39

Connected to electrical grid (%)

Connected to electrical grid: 97
Connected to generators (usually in addition to electrical grid): 77
Poor: 57
Nonpoor: 83

the poor and 21 percent of total expenditure of the nonpoor.[42] Despite the high rate of home ownership, mortgage financing is rare.[43]

Quality of housing

Although expenditure on housing is not particularly high by international standards, the quality of housing purchased is relatively low. Fifty-one percent of Iraqi households live in crowded housing, compared to 54 percent in the Republic of Yemen, 33 percent in the Islamic Republic of Iran, and 1 percent in Jordan.[44] Crowding is particularly severe among the poor—81 percent, compared to 44 percent among the nonpoor. Fourteen percent of the poor live in homes with dirt floors, compared to only 3 percent of the nonpoor.

Road on which the home is located

Iraq's road system was developed in the 1970s and 1980s. Since then, few new roads have been built; existing roads have not been maintained; village feeder roads have been badly neglected; and most war-related damage has gone unrepaired. Most of the population lives on unpaved roads (78 percent of the poor and 65 percent of the nonpoor). Even in urban areas, 66 percent of the poor and 60 percent of the nonpoor live on unpaved roads. Only 15.3 percent of the population lives on paved roads with sidewalks to their dwellings.

Domestic Water and Household Sanitation Services

The quality of water and sanitation infrastructure significantly affects community health—in particular, levels of observed malnutrition (see Annex 7.1). Figure 8.1 and Figure 8.2 illustrate the significant differences in rates of malnutrition among Iraqi children whose homes are served by improved water and sanitation sources, in contrast to those whose homes are not.

---

[42] Poor tenants pay an average of 11,600 dinars per person per month, whereas nonpoor tenants pay an average of 24,800 dinars per person per month. For homeowners (that is, 78.6 percent of the population) the value of housing expenditure was imputed as the market value of the home if it were rented, as determined by the households themselves. Using this method, the average imputed rent of poor homeowners was determined to be 12,700 dinars per person per month. The average imputed rent of nonpoor homeowners was determined to be 31,500 dinars per person per month.

[43] A Quality of Life Survey conducted by the U.S. Agency for International Development found that only 2.8 percent of homeowners had mortgages as of 2004.

[44] Crowding is defined as two or more persons per room. A room is defined as bedrooms, living rooms, and dining rooms but does not include kitchens, bathrooms, or corridors. (Data are from *World Development Indicators:* CD version, 2008.) To allow international comparisons, the crowding numbers stated here are the percent of *households* not individuals.

Figure 8.1. Child Malnutrition: Improved versus Unimproved Water (Percent)

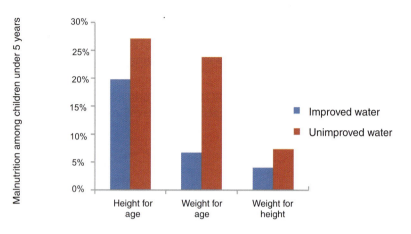

Figure 8.2. Child Malnutrition: Improved versus Unimproved Sanitation (Percent)

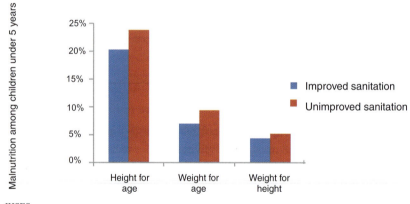

Source: IHSES.

Sources of domestic water

In *urban* areas, connection to the public water system is near universal among both the poor and nonpoor. In *rural* areas, about 38 percent of the poor and just over half the nonpoor are connected to public water supply. Although connection to the public water supply is common, reliability in water delivery is not. Only 9 percent of the poor and 13 percent of the nonpoor report stable supply in water from the public system. Nearly a third report daily interruptions, and another third report weak supply or interruptions more than once a week. Most households must therefore supplement their water supply from secondary sources such as tanker trucks or open wells. In rural areas, 22 percent of those connected to the public network obtain water from rivers and creeks during the frequent interruptions.

Sanitation services

About two-thirds of the poor and 80 percent of the nonpoor are connected to the public sewer network or use a septic tank for sanitation. As with water connections, most differences between the poor and the nonpoor are attributable to residential location rather than to poverty per se. In rural areas, only 51 percent of the poor and 61 percent of the nonpoor use improved sources of sanitation. In urban areas, 79 percent of the poor and 86 percent of the nonpoor use improved sources of sanitation.

Garbage disposal

Fewer than 30 percent of Iraqis (14 percent of the poor and 33 percent of the nonpoor) have municipal garbage collection. The most common means of disposal (55 percent) is to throw garbage into public areas, vacant lots, streets, or open dumps outside the house. In rural areas, 23 percent of residents burn their garbage.

Household Energy

Domestic fuel

The poor and nonpoor devote similar shares of expenditures to fuels (7.3 percent and 8.6 percent). Unlike many other countries, the poor and nonpoor use more or less the same fuels (LPG, kerosene, electricity, benzene, coal, and diesel), and as shown in Figure 8.3, in roughly similar proportions.

Figure 8.3. Fuels Used by the Poor and Nonpoor (Percent)

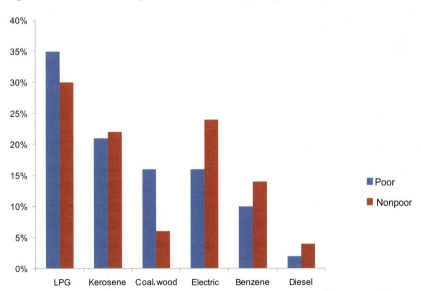

Source: IHSES.

67

At the time of the IHSES field study, consumer prices for domestic fuel were volatile, apparently due to security-related problems affecting distribution. While international prices for Iraq's domestic fuel products rose significantly after 2005, pass-through in the form of higher prices for domestic consumers has been limited. Other than a small subsidy for kerosene, direct budgetary subsidies for fuel were eliminated in 2007. However, indirect subsidies remain sizable at almost 6 percent.

Chapter 9

Transfers

The Size of Iraq's Safety Nets

Transfers account for a large share of Iraqis' income:[45] 28 percent for the poor and 21 percent for the nonpoor. The term *transfer* covers income from a wide range of sources and forms: public and private, cash and in-kind. *Public transfers* include the Public Distribution System (PDS) providing universal food rations and the Social Protection Net (SPN) providing cash transfers targeted to the poor, and pensions. *Private transfers* include gifts from other households, remittances from abroad, traditional *zakat* (alms), and other income from sources such as nongovernmental organizations. The large majority of transfer income (83 percent) comes from public sources, with the remaining 17 percent from private sources (Table 9.1).

Table 9.1. Transfer Income by Poverty Status: Amount (ID per person per month) and Share (Percent)

Indicator	Non-poor	Poor	Iraq
Public transfers			
Rations (PDS)	11,000 (45 %)	11,500 (61%)	11,100 (48%)
Pensions	6,200 (25%)	3,000 (16%)	5,400 (23%)
Social Protection Net (SPN)	300 (1 %)	200 (1%)	300 (1%)
Other public in cash	2,000 (8%)	1,700 (9%)	1,900 (8%)
Other public in kind	300 (1%)	200 (1%)	300 (1%)
Subtotal, public	19,800 (81%)	16,600 (88%)	19,000 (83%)
Private transfers			
Private in cash	3,300 (14%)	1,700 (9%)	2,900 (13%)
Private in kind	1,300 (5%)	600 (3%)	1,100 (5%)
Subtotal, private	4,600 (19%)	2,300 (12%)	4,000 (17%)
Total transfer income	24,300 (100%)	18,900 (100%)	23,100 (100%)

---

[45] Table 5.1 (Chapter 5) shows income from all sources, including income from employment and property as well as from transfers. Recall that the poverty line is defined in terms of expenditures (Chapter 2). Although income is closely related to expenditure, the two indicators are not identical.

Table 9.2. Summary of Transfer Mechanisms

Budgetary costs of public transfers

Food rations from Public Distribution System (PDS)
Amount, 2007: US$3.9 billion   Amount, 2008: US$6.98 billion
Share of overall government budget (2008): 8.6%

Social Protection Net (SPN program, administered by MOLSA)
Amount, 2007: US$0.83 billion   Amount, 2008: US$0.67 billion

Public spending on social safety nets, as a share of GDP (%):
Iraq: 8.8
MENA average: 3.6

Benefits and beneficiaries

Food rations (PDS)
Poor: 99%   Nonpoor: 99%
Average benefit amount: ID 11,100 per person per month
Benefit amount *among recipients*: ID 11,100 per person per month
Benefit amount among recipients as percentage of poverty line: 14%

Social Protection Net (SPN)
Poor: 4%   Nonpoor: 2%
Average benefit amount: ID 300 per person per month
Benefit amount *among recipients*: ID 10,100 per person per month
Benefit amount among recipients as percentage of poverty line: 13%

The importance of food rations (%)

Households with at least 1 food ration card: 99.7
Households that received wheat rations during previous month: 79.1
PDS wheat flour as share of total wheat flour consumption: 55.4
PDS food rations as share of average caloric requirement: 85

Sources: Budget data from the Ministry of Finance (MOF) and Bayt al Hikma and the report of the Food Ration Reform High Committee; other data from IHSES.

Table 9.2 summarizes the absolute amounts and relative shares from various transfer sources. For the poor and nonpoor, rations are the largest source of transfer income, and approximately the same amounts in absolute terms.[46]   The poor receive absolutely and relatively less from both pensions and private transfers.

Iraq spends a great deal on its public safety nets—8.8 percent of GDP for the combined budgets of the rations program (PDS) and the Social Protection Net (SPN) in 2008.[47] Figure 9.1 compares this very high level of spending to that of comparator countries and to other regions of the world. Among the 73 countries for which data are available, only two—Mauritius, and Bosnia and Herzegovina—spend a higher share on safety nets as a share of GDP.

Figure 9.1 Public Spending on Safety Nets as a Share of GDP (Percent)

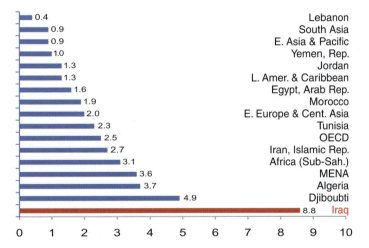

Sources: C. Weigand and M. Grosh, "Levels and Patterns of Safety Net Spending in Developing and Transition Countries," Social Protection Discussion Paper 0817, World Bank, Washington, DC, 2008; data for Iraq updated from Ministry of Finance and Bayt al Hikma to reflect 2008 spending.
Note: OECD refers to Organisation for Economic Co-operation and Development.

---

[46] Although the absolute amounts are the same, rations for the poor account for a relatively larger portion (two-thirds) of their total transfer income. For the nonpoor, rations account for less than half of total transfer income.

[47] As used in Figure 9.1, *safety net* is defined as a noncontributory transfer targeted in some manner to the poor or vulnerable. Some writers use the terms *welfare* and *social assistance* to mean roughly the same thing. The term *safety nets* does not include other forms of social protection—for example, social insurance programs such as pensions and unemployment insurance.

Public Transfers

Public Distribution System

The Public Distribution System was introduced in 1990 in response to the declining supply of food imports under UN-imposed sanctions, and was later expanded under the Oil-for-Food Programme. The PDS provides fixed monthly quantities of 10 commodities. Although there were major delivery delays in 2006, by the time of IHSES data collection in 2007 most households were receiving their ration on time or with only minor delays.

The PDS is enormous by any measure. It reaches 99 percent of the population, providing 85 percent of required calories.[48] The transfer provided by the PDS is worth ID 11,100 per person per month (about 14 percent of the poverty line). The PDS is also extremely expensive. In 2008, it absorbed fully 8.6 percent of government spending—far more than education (6.0 percent) or health (3.4 percent).

Although the PDS is successful in reaching the poor with large transfers, it is very inefficient as a safety net—first, because it is a universal transfer (providing resources to the nonpoor as well as to the poor), and second, because it distorts the domestic food market. The dominant role played by PDS has massively distorted incentives for Iraqi farmers as well as for private food importers, processers, distributors, and retailers. Farmers are of particular concern because they comprise such a large fraction of the rural poor. PDS's vast imports of food staples have driven down food prices and, therefore, incentives for domestic production. In addition, low domestic prices have encouraged the smuggling of staples to be sold outside the country at higher prices.

There is no doubt that some kind of safety net was (and always will be) needed to help support those unable to support themselves. However, one of the most important decisions facing Iraq today is whether the population would be better served if PDS resources were spent differently—for example, on strengthening the poor to earn higher income from their labor.

---

[48] Rations provide an average of 1,998 calories per person per day (based on food actually received by households as recorded in IHSES). The number of required calories is 2,337 for the average Iraqi (see Chapter 2). While rations provide 85 percent of *required* calories, the allotment provides a lower 68 percent of calories *actually consumed* (78 percent among the poor) because most Iraqis consume more than the minimum number of calories. Although the ration provides a large share of calories, it does not provide a balanced diet because fresh products are not included. A study by the Food and Agriculture Organization and World Food Programme in 2003 found that the ration contains 71 percent of recommended protein, 5 percent of vitamin A, and 29 percent of iron intakes.

Various proposals to reform PDS have been put forward in recent years, but lack of data has made it generally difficult to assess their impact. With IHSES data, simulations can now be performed so that the pros and cons of alternative reforms can be weighed. Annex 9.1 discusses technical aspects of several simulation scenarios. Results are briefly summarized here, as well as in Table 9.3 below.[49]

Microsimulations—
The impact of various
PDS reform scenarios,
Annex 9.1

In the medium-term, the reform scenarios assume that the private sector has responded and is providing adequate food supplies to local markets. The assumption is that supplies would be sufficient and there would no major change in market prices. There are three distinct scenarios:

1. *Eliminate the current PDS system without an alternative program.* The current PDS system is so large that its elimination would dramatically reduce the consumption of the poor as well as the nonpoor. In effect, the value of the ration (approximately ID 11,100, see Table 9.2) would be subtracted from the welfare level of the average poor person (ID 61,624) and from the average Iraqi (ID 126,944). In this scenario, the poor would get poorer, and an additional 10.5 percent of the population would fall into poverty.

2. *Introduce targeting by providing larger transfers to fewer people.* A simple targeting mechanism, referred to as geographic targeting,[50] would allocate benefits only to those in geographic areas with high poverty rates.[51] In this scenario, the poverty headcount would be reduced to 18.6 percent, an

---

[49] The simulations presented here do not model problems associated with management of the PDS. All scenarios assume quality of management similar to that of the existing PDS.

[50] Geographic targeting based on the location of residence is particularly popular because of its simplicity. For a brief overview of issues, see for example, D. Coady, M. Grosh, and J. Hoddinott, 'Targeting Outcomes Redux', *World Bank Research Observer* 19 (1): 61–85. (Spring 2004).

We rank the 54 geographic areas used for sampling in the IHSES (18 governorates by their rural areas, governorate centers, and other urban centers) on the basis of their poverty headcount. If we aim to reduce the headcount at a national level, the optimal number of targeted areas is 22. (This optimization reflects the trade-off between the number of poor people covered by the program and the size of the transfer to each beneficiary.) The accuracy of geographic targeting can be improved by further disaggregating the geographic areas. Too fine a disaggregation, however, creates an administrative problem by tempting households to cross geographic boundaries to obtain benefits.

estimated reduction of 4.3 percentage points over the existing universal PDS system.

3.   *Proxy means testing.* Proxy means testing is a targeting mechanism in which eligibility is based on household characteristics associated with poverty. An eligibility score[52] can be calculated through fixed weights assigned to the particular household characteristics. These characteristics must be easy to verify and hard to manipulate. Under this scenario, Iraq's poverty headcount would drop to 15.0 percent, a reduction of 7.9 percentage points.

Table 9.3. Medium-Term Impacts of Eliminating or Targeting the PDS

Policy	Poverty headcount (%)	Poverty gap (%)	Mean monthly PCE (ID 000s)	Mean monthly PCE among the poor (ID 000s)	Monthly per capita transfer to beneficiaries (ID 000s)
Retain the current system without change	22.9	4.5	126.9	61.6	11.1
Eliminate PDS with no compensating measures	34.4	9.1	115.2	56.5	0.0
Replace PDS with geographically targeted cash transfers	18.6	3.6	127.0	62.2	32.9
Replace PDS with proxy-means-tested (PMT) cash transfers	15.0	2.5	127.8	64.1	33.5

Source: IHSES

---

[52] In our microsimulations for Iraq, the preferred specification includes sociodemographic characteristics of the household (household size, age and gender of the head of household, a dependency ratio, and educational attainment of the household head), housing characteristics (whether the house is rented, crowding, materials of the ceiling and floor, quality of the sewage system and of the road leading to the house), geographical location, labor market status of the household head, and whether he/she works in the public sector. If we aim to reduce the headcount at a national level, the threshold for eligibility is set at the 36th percentile of the estimated welfare distribution.

The short-term impact of PDS reform is more difficult to estimate. PDS has dominated the market for many basic foods for nearly 20 years. Retail prices have been suppressed, and along with them, private sector investment in domestic food production as well as the import, processing, storage, and distribution capacity of the private sector. As a result, capacity is limited in many parts of the food supply chain. The short-term impact of PDS reform is likely to be highly sensitive to the timing and sequencing of the reform process, as well as to simultaneous efforts to strengthen capacity throughout the food supply chain. If the private sector supply response is inadequate, shortages of food and corresponding price increases could result.

Food prices are likely to be the main channel through which the poor are affected by potential PDS reforms. While the above scenarios estimate poverty headcount reductions—from 22.9 percent to 18.6 percent with geographic targeting, or reductions even to 15.0 percent with proxy means testing—the expected poverty reduction could be lost or even reversed if basic food prices increase. For example, a 25 percent increase in the price of food ration products with geographic targeting would reduce the headcount only to 21 percent, and proxy means testing only to 17 percent. If prices of food ration products were to rise by 50 percent, the benefits of targeting would be virtually eliminated.[53]

Analysis of PDS reform scenarios thus highlights two crucial issues. On the one hand, more efficient allocation of present PDS resources through targeting could potentially reduce Iraq's current poverty rate from about 23 percent to 15 percent of the population. Reduction in the depth of poverty (Chapter 3) would also be dramatic. On the other hand, reforms must be phased and carefully structured to avoid inflation in food prices that would offset the benefits. To do so, a capable and competitive food supply chain must be developed in parallel.

Social Protection Net

The Ministry of Labor and Social Affairs (MOLSA) introduced a targeted, cash-based Social Protection Net (SPN) in 2004; and by 2007, its budget had grown to US$800 million. Beneficiary households receive, on average, ID 10,100 per person per month (IHSES data) — nearly as much as the value of food ration transfers.[54]

---

[53] If food ration prices increased by 50 percent, geographic targeting could achieve a poverty rate of 23.5 percent of the population and proxy means testing could achieve a poverty rate of 22.3 percent.

[54] Note that SPN benefits are not necessarily given to all members of a household. For analytical purposes, income is assumed to be shared equally among members of a household.

To be effective for poverty reduction, cash transfers must not only be sufficiently large, they must reach a sizeable number of the intended beneficiaries. In this regard, SPN targeting has been problematic. SPN targets individuals belonging to particular groups, including the disabled, orphaned children, divorced or widowed women, married male university students, families of the imprisoned and missing persons, those unable to work due to terrorism, and the internally displaced. However, as shown in Table 9.4, these categories are not good predictors of poverty. For example, widows and divorced women are considerably *less* likely to be poor than the average Iraqi.

Table 9.4. Poverty Rates by Social Protection Net Eligibility Categories

Category	Headcount (Percent)	Poverty gap (Percent)
Iraq, all	22.9	4.5
Unemployed individuals	26.0	5.2
Individuals in households with disabled members	29.4	6.2
Widows or divorced women	18.6	3.6
Totally disabled persons	22.8	4.5
Underage orphans	30.1	4.8
Married students continuing university studies	10.7	1.8
Individuals in households that suffered the death of a working member	22.8	4.5

Source: IHSES

Inappropriate targeting has two separate effects. First, most of the poor are not beneficiaries; and second, many of the beneficiaries are nonpoor. Both effects have happened in the case of SPN. Less that 10 percent of the poor are reached; and about two-thirds of those who receive benefits are not poor. For this reason, the national poverty reduction strategy calls for an improved SPN targeting mechanism (Chapter 10). The objective is to improve the efficiency so that benefits precisely target the population that is otherwise unable to support itself through labor income. [55]

---

[55] The numbers presented here are based on the 2007 IHSES survey. Since the time of the IHSES survey, the SPN has increased the number of beneficiaries. An assessment of the current targeting cannot be performed, however, until the next nationally representative, household expenditure survey.

Pensions

To the extent that pensions deliver benefits that are based on member contributions, they might be thought of as deferred compensation packages for affiliated employees rather than safety nets. On the other hand, pension systems are often characterized by redistribution of income—from one category of workers or citizens to others, or from one generation to another. Considerable actuarial data would be needed to estimate the extent of such redistributive transfers, and these data are not currently available. We do know, however, that pension income on average accounts for 16 percent of transfer income to the poor, as well as 25 percent to the nonpoor. For individuals living in households that receive pensions, this income is substantial—ID 12,800 per person per month in poor households and ID 22,200 per person per month in nonpoor households.

Pensions and other job benefits, Annex 9.2

The poor in Iraq are almost as likely to benefit from pension income as are the nonpoor. Twenty-three percent of poor Iraqis live in households that receive pension income, compared to 28 percent of nonpoor households.[56] Poor female-headed households are significantly more likely to receive pension income, reflecting the large share of widows among this group. Those in urban areas (both poor and nonpoor) are more likely to receive pension income than their rural counterparts.

Like other systems in the region, the Iraqi pension system faces structural problems that compromise its financial sustainability, reduce economic efficiency, and create intra- and intergenerational inequalities. The following three issues are of particular importance.

First, provisions differ between schemes, with civil servants receiving more generous benefits than others, creating inherent inequalities. The existence of multiple systems also drives up administrative costs and can hinder the movement of the work force, thus precluding efficient allocation of labor—creating a drag on development of the private sector and income growth.

---

[56] Pensions are paid to individuals, but we assume the income is shared within the household. The amount received by the average poor pension recipient is ID 132,300 per month and ID 145,000 per month for the average nonpoor pension recipient. Among the elderly, the nonpoor are significantly more likely to receive pension benefits: 36 percent of the nonpoor aged 65 and over receive pensions compared to only 22 percent of the poor in the same age bracket.

Second, mandates for these systems are unsustainable because they would require gross replacement rates close to 100 percent of the final salary received by the average full-career worker. These are among the highest rates observed in the region. As a result, the pension systems are gradually accumulating unsustainable liabilities from misalignment among the contribution rates, the targeted replacement rates, and the retirement age. Accrued-to-date pension liabilities with current contributors—that is, excluding the liabilities related to current retirees—are estimated at over 60 percent of GDP. This is due, in part, to recent salary increases for civil servants. The contribution rate necessary to equilibrate the old-age pension component (that is, without taking into account disability and survivorship pensions) would need to be set at over 30 percent of the covered wage—a level of taxation that could cause severe loss in competitiveness and the demand for labor.

Finally, the low coverage rate is an additional cause for concern. As pointed out in Chapter 5, only 15 percent of poor workers are covered by the pension system.[57]

Private Transfers

Lending and borrowing, Annex 9.3

Private transfers[58] include gifts from other Iraqi households, remittances from abroad, *zakat*, and income from other kinds of private sources such as NGOs. As shown in Table 9.5, about one-quarter of poor persons receive some amount of private transfers from other households within Iraq, an average of ID 6,900 per person per month. A similar share of the nonpoor receive private transfers from households within Iraq, although they receive about twice as much as the poor (ID 13,500). As illustrated, very few Iraqis receive remittances from abroad—only 2 percent of the poor and 5 percent of the nonpoor.[59]

---

[57] Recall also that employment rates are very low in Iraq. The low coverage rates combined with low employment rates imply that a low share of the total population will benefit from the pension systems.

[58] Only cash and in-kind gifts are considered here. Detailed information on lending and borrowing, another form of private transfer, is reported in Annex 9.3.

[59] Other private transfers, including traditional *zakat*, provide only a trickle of resources, even for their recipients. Among those poor households who receive a positive amount, other private transfers average only ID 1,100 per person per month.

Table 9.5. Private Transfers: Share Received, Amount Received, and Origin, by Poverty Status

Indicator	Share of population (%) receiving private transfers from:			Average amount of these transfers (ID 1,000 / person / month) from:		
	Households inside Iraq	Households outside Iraq	Other private sources	Households inside Iraq	Households outside Iraq	Other private sources
Poor	25	2	33	6.9	7.0	1.1
Nonpoor	23	5	21	13.5	17.9	2.2

Source: IHSES

Among poor households, female-headed households are significantly more likely to receive private transfers than male-headed households, and the amounts received are relatively larger (Table 9.6).

Table 9.6. Private Transfers by Gender of Head of Household

Indicator	Share (%) received from:		Average amount (ID 1,000 / person / month) from:	
	Households inside Iraq	Households outside Iraq	Households inside Iraq	Households outside Iraq
Poor female-headed households	38	7	19.7	20.7
Poor male-headed households	24	2	10.8	15.9

Source: IHSES

Whether male or female-headed, two poor households at the same level of PCE are by definition equally "needy." However, despite being no more needy, female-headed households on average receive larger gifts from other households. This is probably because female-headed households are often (incorrectly) assumed to be poorer than male-headed households (or otherwise more deserving). In fact, the extra support that female-headed households receive may help explain why female-headed households are not poorer than male-headed households.

The transfers that are discussed in this chapter are mostly public. Measured as a share of GDP, the Iraq safety net (that is, PDS rations and SPN transfers) is among the largest in the world. By contrast, private transfers account for only a small share of total transfers received. But though it is large, the Iraqi safety net is not efficient.

PDS rations are the main component of the public system, and thoughtful food ration reform has considerable potential to reduce poverty. Resources that are inefficiently used by PDS could be targeted on interventions that enhance productivity rather than subsidize consumption. This might include interventions such as better general education, skills training, rural roads, agricultural marketing services, electricity provision, and private-sector infrastructure that would create jobs, as well as the strengthening of safety nets that protect those who are unable to earn enough from work. However, food ration reform must be done carefully, first making sure the supply of food in local markets is sufficient. If not, food prices will rise, wiping out the gains that might otherwise be realized.

The SPN is currently ineffective because of poor targeting. Better targeting could make SPN a useful program for protecting those who are unable to earn decent livelihoods from work.

Chapter 10

National Strategy for Poverty Reduction

From the 1980s onward, government spending in Iraq financed the military at the expense of public services and infrastructure. The economy outside the oil sector and the productive activities of the population were largely ignored, with universal food subsidies offered as a palliative. Previous progress was all but wiped out, average income fell, and households became less able to provide for themselves.

The present study has its roots in 2004 when international donors convened to channel and coordinate reconstruction resources. No nationwide income and expenditure surveys had been conducted in more than 20 years, and the need for thorough updating of socioeconomic information was widely recognized. The goal of the Household Survey and Policies for Poverty Reduction Project (HSPPR), therefore, was to institutionalize governmental capacity in data collection, economic analysis, and evidence-based policy making, thereby laying the groundwork for successful implementation of a long-term poverty reduction strategy.

The year-long Iraq Household Socio-Economic Study (IHSES), which was carried out systematically through the civil violence that peaked in 2006–07, produced a high-quality database representing more than 120,000 individuals. These data provided the foundation for the present poverty analysis, which in turn provided the foundation for the National Strategy for Poverty Reduction. The poverty analysis was developed concurrently and iteratively with formation of the strategy, each process strengthening and reinforcing the other.

The present poverty analysis in 2009–10, a historic moment in which Iraq is entering a new phase in its political, economic, and social history. The National Strategy for Poverty Reduction was officially adopted by the Council of Ministers on November 24, 2009, and presented to the Council of Representatives on January 19, 2010. The strategy represents a significant milestone—a clear shift in spending priorities from subsidizing the population's consumption to enabling the poor to earn higher incomes from their labor, and ultimately, to raise living standards in a diversified, stable economy.

Already, the draft 2010 budget takes a step in this direction by directing an increased share of allocations toward human capital development, and the draft National Development Plan has incorporated many of the investments recommended by the National Strategy for Poverty Reduction. Progress on budget alignment, program implementation, and poverty reduction will be monitored through annual reports, including further rounds of IHSES and updates of the poverty analysis. The international community, including the World Bank, will make use of the National Strategy for Poverty Reduction in setting priorities for assistance to Iraq and will provide technical assistance for the strategy's implementation and monitoring.

Table 10.1 summarizes key analytic findings underpinning the six areas of action under the National Strategy for Poverty Reduction.

The National Strategy for Poverty Reduction—Assumptions, partners, and activities,
Annex 10

Table 10.1. Main Findings and Areas of PRS Action

Analysis findings	Key PRS actions and goals

Higher income for the poor from work

Low income is not primarily a problem of unemployment. Rather it is primarily attributable to low-productivity work performed by the poor and the low quality in the education that they receive. A large share of the poor are engaged in the informal sector (nonwage self-employment and wage work in small private businesses) and do not receive job benefits.	The PRS focuses on improving the productivity of the poor. Since poverty is largely a rural phenomenon and a high share of the impoverished work in agriculture on family farms, the strategy emphasizes agricultural extension services and rural infrastructure for production and marketing. Access to credit, which is very constricted in Iraq, is to be widened. Stronger labor law enforcement is called for. Opportunities are to be opened for adults to upgrade their skill sets to compensate for the inadequate educations they received as children.

Table 10.1. continued

Improved health status

The quality of public health care is low, pushing the poor toward private providers at very high prices. Substandard water and sanitation causes health problems, including malnutrition. The poor rely heavily on the food ration, which by itself is not nutritionally adequate. The poor have low-quality reproductive health care and have very high fertility rates. The high fertility rates exacerbate poverty by increasing the economic dependency ratio and reducing female labor force participation.

Improve public health care by upgrading staff training, equipment, and facilities. Expand water and sanitation to poor areas. Maintain food rations for the poor and reintroduce school feeding programs that are nutritionally balanced. (Note that school feeding programs also are expected to raise student attendance rates.) Improve the quality of reproductive health care through steps that include staff training, provision of medical supplies, and public awareness campaigns.

Upgrading of education

The quality of the education system is low, as evidenced by the low returns to education. Attendance rates are low, particularly among the poor in rural areas, and they drop markedly at the intermediate level. Poor farmers have high rates of illiteracy and correspondingly low productivity.

Extend compulsory education to the intermediate level. Increase budget allocation to improve educational quality, with priority given to provision of educational materials, school building rehabilitation, and teacher training in poor areas. Link SPN benefits to school attendance. Provide literacy programs for poor adults. Provide vocational education programs for poor adults to improve their marketable skills.

Better living environments

The poor live in overcrowded, low-quality housing. A large share live on unpaved roads and lack access to garbage removal services.

Expand the supply of affordable housing, with an emphasis on incentives for the private sector. Expand coverage of paved roads, garbage collection, and other public services in poor areas.

(continued next page)

Table 10.1. continued

Effective social protection

The main safety net program in Iraq, the Public Distribution System (PDS), provides a universal ration that absorbs a large part of the government budget because it is not targeted to the poor. Because the PDS has dominated food markets, reform must be carefully handled to ensure adequate private sector supply response. (If the supply response is inadequate, food shortages and inflation will result. Because such a large share of the population lives just above the poverty line, shocks such as food inflation could dramatically increase poverty rates.) The Social Protection Net (SPN) is not well targeted: many poor people do not benefit from it and many of the beneficiaries are not poor.

Establish a reform process for the PDS that would include targeting the system to the poor. Transfer savings from a better targeted PDS to increase benefits of priority programs. Develop an effective targeting mechanism for the SPN that is based on the official poverty line. Improve SPN management, including development of a functional database of beneficiaries and expanded staff training. Launch a public awareness campaign to disseminate information about eligibility criteria.

Reduced inequality between men and women

Female labor force participation is exceptionally low, as is school attendance among poor girls.

Provide vocational training programs and awareness-raising campaigns to encourage income-generating activities among women. Increase awareness and enforcement of the rights of female workers. Design and conduct awareness campaigns to increase school enrollment rates among girls.

Sources and Background Papers

Unless otherwise noted in the text, statistics cited in this report refer to IHSES data analysis (see the supplementary reference volume); or in some cases, the IHSES Tabulation Report (2008). Researchers can obtain data disks from www.cosit.gov.iq or http://go.worldbank.org/pw5wdschz0. Other sources are generally cited in the preceding text or corresponding footnotes. More extensive documentation from the secondary literature and from other statistical sources can be found in six substantive background papers that were prepared by teams of Iraqi content experts and officials working in related areas. Their papers were first prepared in autumn 2008 and discussed at an initial analysis seminar in January 2009. The papers and teams that produced them are as follows:

Poverty from the Gender Perspective
Dr. Mehdi Muhsin Al-Alak
Hussain Mansour Hussain
Dr. Nahida Abdulkarim
Thanaa Abbas Salman
Ayad Jawad Hassan
Firyal Mahmood

Education and Poverty
Dr. Abida Ahmed Dakhil
Dr. Ali Shidakh Al-AZubaidy
Nawal Abbas Mehdi
Eqood Hussain Salman
Dr. Ahmed Al-Hussaini
Basma Abdulwahab

Income and Expenditure
Dr. Amira Mohammed Hussain
Dr. Abdullah Al-Bandar
Riyadh Fakher Khalaf
Dr. Qussai Al-Jabiri
Nidhal Abdulkarim Jawad
Najlaa Ali Murad
Dalia Abdul Lateef
Fadhil Nauookh

Poverty Impact on Health
Dr. Ihsan Jaafar Ahmed
Dr. Mona Atalla Ali
Dr. Faris Hassan Al-Lami
Khawla Al Mohammed
Bushra Nasif Jassim

Manpower, Employment, and Poverty
Zaki Abdulwahab Al-Jadir
Dr. Wafaa Jaafar Al-Mahdawi
Mahmood Othman
Abdulla Hassan Mathi
Sundus Jawad Hussain
Qussai Abdulfatah Raoof

The Role of the Social Network
Alaa Abdulla Mahmood
Layla Kadim Aziz
Dr. Abdulwahid Moshal
Najah Jalil Khalil
Bassima Mohammed Sadiq
Nada Ahmed Ameen

Contents of Reference Materials Volume

The reference materials in the supplementary volume are all available electronically in both Arabic and English. They can be downloaded at no charge from the World Bank (www.worldbank.org/iq) or COSIT websites (www.cosit.gov.iq).